The Web3 Era

The Web3 Era

NFTs, the Metaverse, Blockchain, and the Future of the Decentralized Internet

David Shin

WILEY

This edition first published 2023

© 2023 John Wiley & Sons, Ltd.

Registered Offices

John Wiley & Sons, Inc., 111 River Street, Hoboken, NJ 07030, USA

John Wiley & Sons Ltd, The Atrium, Southern Gate, Chichester, West Sussex, PO19 8SQ, UK

Editorial Office

John Wiley & Sons Singapore Pte. Ltd. 134 Jurong Gateway Road, #04-307H Singapore 600134

For details of our global editorial offices, customer services, and more information about Wiley products visit us at www.wiley.com.

Wiley also publishes its books in a variety of electronic formats and by print-on-demand. Some content that appears in standard print versions of this book may not be available in other formats.

Library of Congress Cataloging-in-Publication Data is Available:

ISBN 9781119983934 (Cloth)
ISBN 9781119983941 (ePDF)
ISBN 9781119983958 (ePub)

Cover Design: Courtesy of Chris Koo Cover Image: © CKA/Shutterstock Author photo: Courtesy of David Shin
Printed and bound by CPI Group (UK) Ltd, Croydon, CR0 4YY

C9781119983934_270223

CONTENTS

INTRODUCTION

As a child of immigrant parents growing up in Toronto, Canada, I saw a lot in terms of the hardships that moving to a new country can bring to a family. Especially when English as a second language did not exist. So for my parents to learn a new language and culture in their forties while focused on subsistence for the family, it was a lot to take in.

The one bright spot was the community they were a part of at that time. A small Korean community of other immigrants started to form around a Christian church. This gave my parents a way to escape from the daily grind of life as an immigrant in Canada and remember the common things that they shared with like-minded people who had similar upbringings.

This is where my story starts – communities and how they played a part in my early childhood to how they developed me as an adolescent and then a full-grown adult.

Music was a big part of life after my father passed away when I was 12 years old, and the concerts

I attended when I was still in high school are formative experiences I've had growing up. One of the bands I listened to often and enjoyed going to see was the Grateful Dead. I still enjoy dropping a few of their greatest tracks on my Spotify playlist and cranking up the volume. . .

The folklore, which the band adopted in their name, of the virtuous traveler who comes across the corpse of a man who died without paying his debts still strikes me as one of the noblest lessons in humanity. Spending every last penny to give the man a proper burial, the traveler is saved from an impossible situation at the end of the story, by the spirit of the deceased.

Attending their concerts, I learned quickly how the band's fanbase worked. It was all about building and participating in a community environment. Like the hippie era of the 1960s and 1970s, everything was shared and everything was about the atmosphere and energy that came with being a "Dead Head." Experiencing this during my high school years played a tremendous role on how I looked at communities and the value that a strong community can bring to the commercialization of music, a product, a service, and even a group of people.

As I got into university and became more academically curious, craving more knowledge and insight, I picked up a book that would change the way I think forever. Che Guevara's biography had a profound effect on how I viewed the world. I was always curious as to why a well-educated Argentinian who came from a good middle-class family risked his life to fight a war that was not his – the Cuban war.

As I learned, he was impacted during his travels in Latin America by the poor and underserved people of the countries he traveled through. He felt a strong sense of injustice and inequality across the different Latin American societies. His experiences eventually evolved to standing up to political bullies and fighting a revolution for these people who did not have a voice, who could not stand up for themselves to improve their lives.

However, others may interpret Che Guevara's plight, this is how I viewed it and formed my opinion. Perhaps it was because of the similar inequality that I witnessed growing up with my parents, having to deal with a lot as immigrants in Canada. Regardless, my thoughts were clear and I had an overwhelming conviction that if I could one day contribute to the overall improvement of society in a way that can create balance, particularly from a financial standpoint, I was going to do this and make it my life's mission.

Fast forward to adulthood, having this mission as a young university student, I felt convinced I would change the world. However, the reality was that I needed to make a career for myself and evolve as an individual with marriage and children as a point of reference. After graduating from the University of Waterloo, I took it upon myself to get a good paying job, get married, and start building a family as soon as I could. Thinking back on it now, I believe I had a sense of urgency to do all this as I saw my father passed away at the age of 50. I believe this had a profound effect, although more subconsciously, to do things quicker in life.

Getting married at the age of 28, taking on incredible opportunities in banking overseas and having children by the age of 32, I felt like life was moving in the right direction. However, I always had an itch to do more in the world and a fascination about how I could one day move the needle somehow when it came to those who needed help the most in society. I just needed to find that intersection in life that would allow me to be a contributor in doing that, which came several years later while I was having a conversation at a bar with a friend who was also in banking.

It was February 2012, and a friend working at another bank asked me, "Have you heard about this thing called Bitcoin?" My life would change forever from that point onward. I remember I went home that night and googled Bitcoin. The first thing that popped up was Satoshi Nakamoto's white paper. I read the white paper and could not fall asleep that night. I had fallen down the proverbial rabbit hole. It was a feeling like no other.

As if I was now "woke," clearly seeing what the future could look like in finance, I was compelled to believe my calling was in doing something with Bitcoin. As I took more and more time to learn about how the blockchain worked and how Bitcoin, as a new store of value, could revolutionize the banking sector let alone the world, I started to focus on how I could increase more awareness and, ultimately, adoption of the technology. This led me down the path of meeting like-minded Bitcoin enthusiasts in Hong Kong, where I was based at the time.

Meeting other Bitcoin believers in Hong Kong really had an impact on my own belief that it would be communities and not mass adoption that would start the early phase of its growth in Asia. One day in early 2013, I asked several Bitcoin Meetup friends to gather by the pier at the Hong Kong Ferry Terminal. In my hand, I had a presentation for all four people who were there: Aurelien Menant, Arthur Hayes, Larry Salibra, and a young Leo Weese.

The front cover of the presentation had the title, "Friends of Satoshi." This presentation outlined how the five of us were going to set up and create the very first Bitcoin association in Hong Kong/Asia. It had high-level goals for what the association wanted to achieve and it set forth what would be required to achieve these goals. The last page of the presentation outlined the roles and responsibilities of the founding members who were all huddled together at the pier that fateful evening.

It was from that night onward that the Bitcoin Association of Hong Kong (BAHK) was formed. We hired a lawyer out of Taiwan who was willing to accept Bitcoin as payment to help draft the BAHK's legal constitution. We approached an agency to help with the setup of the legal entity and as the weeks and months went on, the association started to grow with more and more community members signing up to our meetups, events, and eventually conferences. It currently is one of the largest not-for-profit associations in Asia and is one of the key groups that the Hong Kong government and regulators turn to for guidance on industry best practices and regulation. Community building and growth is tantamount to the success of any emerging technology. Without a core community of developers, users, and investors, crypto and blockchain would not have moved as quickly as it has over the last 10 years.

As an early adopter of Bitcoin and other crypto assets, I have had the distinct privilege of being a part of many interesting discussions about the use and application of digital currencies including conversations with regulators, financial institutions, central banks, and family offices. Due to the disruptive nature of digital assets to banking and the global markets, traditional financial organizations had to pay attention to market valuations, trade volumes, mainstream adoption, and the progress of open-source development in the crypto space. Just like Microsoft didn't take Linux for corporate adoption seriously or IBM didn't take Apple seriously for personal computing, traditional finance needed to have one hand on the steering wheel when it came to the development of the crypto industry and the speed at which the infrastructure was being built.

Through the various engagements, particularly with the central banks, I was able to learn early on that digital assets would soon also be a political topic as it seemed that more and more countries looked at blockchain and Central Bank Digital Currencies (CBDCs) as an alternative to cross-border SWIFT settlements in global trade. This also helped shape my thoughts on the importance of asset-backed currencies versus government-backed currencies and how in the near future "under-banked highly commoditized" countries could leverage digital assets as a means to settle trades between countries that are not as developed as the G7 nations. There is a big opportunity in how this technology could be used in places like Africa, Southeast Asia, and Latin America, where the unbanked with an entry-level smartphone, an internet connection and a digital wallet that connects to a blockchain, could be offered simple banking tools to be integrated into the wider financial system, ultimately improving lives and growing their local economies.

The journey thus far has been an incredible one, full of ups and downs, but it's my long-term view of the industry that keeps me believing in the ultimate success of it all. The idea of decentralization and mass adoption of distributed ledgers over the internet by governments and institutions felt like a pipe dream several years ago. As blockchains and their use cases continue to advance from Bitcoin as a digital store of value to Ethereum as digital legal agreements to non-fungible tokens (NFTs) representing intellectual property rights on chain, to the financialization of the gaming industry, it is important to note that without progressive regulation the overall growth and success is limited. Regulation is key to ensure faith in the system and to keep those building products and services on chain accountable.

The trick is to ensure that regulators also evolve in terms of their policies and that they engage industry thought leaders in open communication to derive best practices that are implementable and that don't stifle innovation. Regulation should not slow industries down like brakes in a car but, rather, they should look and feel more like a seat belt. Safety, fairness, and transparency should be the tenets of how a framework for regulating the crypto industry could work.

With borders reopening in the post-Covid era, attracting top tech talent is a key focus for many countries trying to build and expand their tech sector, which is more reason for regulators in these markets to ensure a pragmatic and progressive approach when developing crypto policies.

I hope to educate as many as possible with this book. It highlights the pivotal points in political, economic, social, and religious history where human civilization took turns for better or for worse, ultimately bringing us to the world we know today that is ruled by the strongest nations, while looking toward the future and the technology that will break us free from the cycles of oppression.

I hope you treat this book as a learning journey. It has been one for me.

1 Rise of the DAOs

From the dawn of humanity, *Homo sapiens* have formed alliances. Starting with the first groups of nomadic hunter-gatherers to ancient agricultural civilizations, it is evident that we need each other to survive and thrive.

From family units to communities, early humans had their individual roles to play to make a society work and the more diversified they were, the faster their society progressed. There were checks and balances in place to ensure that we did not have too many people doing the same job as resources were already scarce, not to mention it took years to be a proficient hunter with primitive tools, and probably longer for gatherers to identify all the species of edible flora that would not kill them.

As we grew larger in numbers through agriculture, leadership was needed. But instead of dividing the task of leading, in the heat of constant wars in an age where *might is right*, kings were crowned and dynasties ruled with the power kept solely in their bloodlines.

When citizens realized a new form of governance was needed, the idea of nation states was born. Led by leaders elected through a democratic process of voting, balance would finally be restored. This provided levels of governance under people who were chosen by us. Now, we could all decide on our own future by electing our own leader who would act in the best interest of the country and majority, or so we thought. . .

After two world wars and countless conflicts, genocides, and human rights atrocities, it is clear that whatever system of governance we have trusted is not enough. According to the 2016 Edelman Trust Barometer, half the world population distrusts the government. It is not hard to see why.

The elected officials in power who were sworn to protect us act in the best interest of big business and themselves. As evident from reports on Wikileaks, and exposés on the likes of the Panama and Pandora Papers, those with influence hide their wealth in the offshore accounts of shell companies. According to the BBC, The Pandora Papers leak alone includes 6.4 million documents, almost three million images, more than one million emails, and almost half-a-million spreadsheets pertaining to 330 politicians from 90 countries who use secret offshore companies to hide their wealth.

The power structure has, until today, been a pyramid with a few sitting on top. We are no longer in an age where *might is right*. It is not the nations with the biggest guns that will rule the world, it is the nations with the biggest GDPs that will inherit significant veto power and sit at the head of the table of international negotiations. Cash, with its explicable ability to bend the will of nations today, is king.

Likewise, many of us have the same thing in mind. Make enough money so we can retire and enjoy life at whatever age we target. It used to be by age 40, if you're ambitious. Today, some of Gen Z are doing it before hitting 20.

Cash is driving us to act as individuals instead of as a community. We all want what's best for ourselves and are willing to get it at the expense of others, whether knowingly or not. It is the circle of pain that consumerism and capitalism have trapped us in and if we don't find a way out, our children will suffer the same fate.

There are eight billion of us in the world today. Humans just keep growing in numbers despite the scarcity of resources and global warming; however, according to scientists working for the United Nations, we have nearly peaked in our numbers.

Due to the competitive, high-consuming nature of our lives, the global population is predicted to grow to 8.5 billion by 2030. After that, it will slightly increase to 8.97 billion by 2300. This is a far cry from the boom of billions of new souls we saw in the last two centuries, brought about by breakthroughs in medical science that made certain diseases and health risks, like the act of giving birth, a thing of the past.

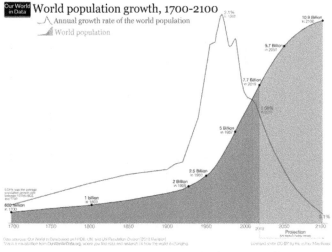

Source: Ourworldindata / https://ourworldindata.org/world-population-growth / last accessed December 08, 2022 / CC BY 4.0.

The flattening of the curve in our population growth is more than just a telling sign that there is something wrong with the world today. Maybe that is why sustainability has been the buzzword for the past decade. As it is, we are looking at extended periods of drought that will disrupt food supplies. What more when it comes to fuel and other mineral shortages? What about the world's depleting freshwater supply?

Often, the most vulnerable in our societies will suffer the consequences of our actions and it is ironic that democracy and the vote were supposed to ensure that no one gets left behind.

The answers to our most concerning questions are not being addressed or taken seriously enough by leaders, and anyone who challenges the status quo gets reprimanded, jailed, or even executed, by the state.

It seems that no matter how many seas we sail across, how many new lands we discover, or how many flags we raise, we will always have a problem with leadership.

King for a Day

We feel safe when we believe we have a capable leader who can defend us from threats, whether from invading forces or waning job markets and a weak economy.

When *might was right*, leaders were also commanders of great armies who had proven themselves on the battlegrounds. A nation felt safe in the hands of ex-military men such as Winston Churchill, Napoleon Bonaparte, or Mustafa Kemal Atatürk. But in times of peace, people return to voting for the candidate who can promise a brighter future or, at least, stability.

Winning an election is essentially a game of numbers but if we look past the divisive politics used to gain votes, most people just want stability. Hence, we want to see the results before making decisions, so based on past records the most credible person is often chosen.

The Guardian interviewed six Donald Trump voters during his first campaign for presidency of the United States and among the reasons given for voting for Trump was because they wanted "more conservative laws," and believed he could make deals that will make America prosperous again and renew the American Dream.

As an outsider, he wasn't a politician. He was a blank canvas and as a reality TV star, he could be many things to different people – he could stoke racial and religious tensions with Islamophobia and anti-immigrant fascism with his Mexican border wall idea, while selling the notion of voters as the ones to Make America Great Again.

The act of deciding on a course of action is a double-edged sword. Make the right decision, get praised, and reap the rewards for the outcome, likewise, make the wrong decision and bear the blame. Despite his loud antics in his debate with Joe Biden, Trump's true persona was revealed that night to a very much different America – an America that had been torn by conflicts it could no longer hide.

Trump's refusal to criticize Proud Boys, a radical right-wing militant group amid the on-going Black Lives Matters, and his denial of the inadequacy of his administration's response to COVID-19, did not sit well with Americans. Whatever faces Trump wore while charismatically speaking to voters at rallies, melded into one and revealed a person who was only looking out for himself.

If you need an even more harrowing example of how a leader can mislead a nation, Adolf Hitler himself once said, "I use emotion for the many and reserve reason for the few."

This has happened across the globe throughout history – we've elected what we perceived as strong leaders, who some even revere as godlike, only to find out they are fallible humans just like the rest of us.

How can we trust anyone, when we can't even trust ourselves?

The best that we can hope for is that we choose leaders who know what they are doing. So we elect leaders who surround themselves with subject matter experts who aren't always acting in our best interest and are limited by bureaucracy. They, in turn, surround themselves with other sub-experts and the cycle goes on. Before you know it, another traditionally structured organization is born. Whoopee.

This brings us back to square one: small, elite groups of people who decide the fate of the world.

Can we continue to trust these people to steer us in the right direction?

Does Your Vote Really Count?

Voting on a mass scale has never been an easy task to execute. Nations spend millions of dollars running general elections every four or five years to choose a leader or ruling party from the same pool of candidates. And nothing ever changes.

The idea of voting is great. In practice, however, it doesn't work so well.

Voting gave us the right to elect our own leaders but through vote tampering, gerrymandering, party hopping, control of media and propaganda, and outright bribery, less than desirable leaders stay in power for extended periods of time – even amending laws to prolong their dictatorships. If this is the best democracy can do, it needs to be fixed.

In fact, the world seems more divided now more than ever. And despite all the technology we have to stay connected, we just can't seem to understand each other due to the use of social media to disseminate propaganda and fake news to stoke tensions.

Millions or even billions of voices – many uninformed – spoil the outcome. The human traits of selfishness and competitiveness will always get the better of us and cloud our judgment. Remember what Hitler said about using emotions to control the masses?

In addition, use of the ballot box was largely limited to politics due to the manpower needed to execute the count, and the transparency and credibility required by all voters to accept the outcome as legitimate. As such, large-scale voting is usually limited to elections of politicians to lead a nation. Only a few of us around the world have the right to vote for our local council persons, and fewer still when it comes to other local governance officials.

Imagine what we could achieve if we changed the system, most people are already thinking of this – how to evolve past the system of ballot voting that we're stuck in.

If we could just gain trust again, and turn voting into a natural act, we could technically vote on anything and everything.

Imagine a world where experts could converge and vote on the best course of action with total transparency, and seamlessly. Imagine what if the right groups of people came together, found the best solutions, and voted for the right answers to the world's problems.

Now, imagine that these groups of people were not from the same country and weren't bound by any agendas apart from their own desire to see a better future.

Sounds like something out of a science fiction movie, but the foundations of this new system are being laid out now as we speak.

What a Wonderful, Trustless World

Can we have a nation without a leader? How about a company with no CEO or a school with no principal or headmaster?

The most successful groups of people in this world are probably musicians. They come together with a common goal – to create music, and don't overlap each other in abilities – how many times have you seen a band with four drummers?

Maybe that was the world that Louis Armstrong meant when he sang "What a Wonderful World." A trustless world. A place where everyone has something specific to do, and they do it right. A place where we wouldn't need to question the outcome, where we could just trust the system.

If we could get everyone to do their part and remove the issue of trust, humanity would leap forward.

Decentralized Autonomous Organizations, or DAOs, are the next evolution in internet communities. Drawing back to the days of early tribalism, DAOs are groups of people driven by common goals. These new-age tribes are essentially decentralized in power. There is no leader, each member is a leader.

But what about the problem of having too many voices?

By staking something or bringing more value, a member of a DAO receives more tokens, which will

give them more power to vote, participate, and steer
the direction of the group. What value they bring to
the group could be in the form of experience or
qualification – or how much they stake financially. In
theory, there could be various levels of power in a DAO
according to how many tokens a person has but each
level of authority will be verified through what the
person brings to the table. Likewise, there could be no
limit to how many top-level decision makers there are,
hence solving the problem of a few individuals deciding
the outcome of many.

What we have right now with our current internet
(Web 2.0) is a platform where people converge with
moderators and admins – be it an actual person looking
through what everyone is saying or a Facebook bot
picking up violations to community guidelines. Much
like the real world, there is no failsafe if people pull out
of agreements or deals go bad or even if vote
tampering happens.

But we are entering into a Web 3.0 world shaped
by blockchain.

Blockchain technology changed the way
accountability could be handled with full transparency.
Although it started with the original cryptocurrency,
Bitcoin, the technology has grown from just a way to
verify transactions using anonymous servers that then
added the records to a digital ledger. If Bitcoin
decentralized money with blockchain, then Ethereum

decentralized the world with a blockchain that was adaptable through programming smart contracts.

Smart contracts are programs stored on a blockchain that perform functions when predetermined conditions are met. As we are still in the early years of blockchain, smart contracts are typically used to execute an agreement autonomously, instantaneously, and without any third parties except for the blockchain verifying the outcome.

In a DAO, everything is automated and run by smart contracts. Think of it as the agreements made by the original founders of the DAO. These agreements are dictated by the desired outcome of the DAO.

Communication between DAO members may or may not be necessary, depending on the objective of the DAO. But in theory, a DAO is run by humans who use computers to verify their governance of the group. From proposing to voting, the function of a DAO is controlled by servers that validate data and keep things transparent.

Unlimited by distance, the doctors of the world could form a DAO, and so could lawyers, architects, engineers, or even musicians across the globe. And they could come together to find a vaccine, create new laws, build cities that address global warming better, or invent new genres of music (and create an automated way to market it as a non-fungible token, or NFT). Voting in these tribes will be fully automated, run with smart contracts powered by blockchain technology, eliminating the issue of trust.

It is most likely that you will be a member of a DAO sometime in the near future. Even if it is for a purpose as mundane as deciding what music gets played more on the radio – which might be a free-stake DAO that is just run by how often you stream and share music and your agreement to sharing your data.

Why the First DAO Had to Fall

The first DAO, simply known as The DAO, started as a way for investors to autonomously invest ETH. It got hacked and a total of 30% of users' funds (US$60 million) were lost.

The idea for The DAO was first born in 2015 by a team of developers called Slock.it to raise funds for various Web 3.0 projects and startups. They built a smart contract for crowdfunding and programmed voting rights and ownership. The DAO was launched less than a year later in May 2016 to much hype. People were excited that the future of organizations could actually be decentralized. It was, in all sincerity, the first truly decentralized, autonomous, and community-run fund in history.

As expected, everyone rushed to join The DAO and staked their ETH. The DAO raised an unimaginable amount for a new conception and something so abstract at the time. US$150 million (based on the value of Ethereum in June 2016) was collected from members of The DAO and placed in the group's fund.

The DAO did not last long. It's quick success and decline is perhaps a reminder not to take new technology for granted, or to avoid *FOMO*, fear of missing out.

Similar to investing in a company, investors placed money into The DAO with the hope that their shares, or tokens in this case, would appreciate in value.

Instead of the executive decisions that majority shareholders in a traditional company get, in a DAO, you have control over the organization's collected assets based on how many governance tokens you hold.

In addition, if you own any reputable amount of tokens, then you can draft any type of proposal to which the rest of the DAO's community will vote on. Examples of proposals in The DAO's case could be to invest a portion of the group's funds into emerging blockchain startups or flipping NFTs for profit.

Being the first isn't always a good thing. And for The DAO, ambition clearly clouded the group as the rise in value of The DAO's market capitalization and other hyped-up news about its bright future blinded the community from messages on various chat boards written by programmers who warned of code vulnerabilities in The DAO's smart contracts.

Not long after The DAO's formation, hackers exploited the vulnerabilities and siphoned more than half of The DAO's funds before a portion, but not everything, was returned. The lesson was clear. Cash got the better of The DAO. However, The DAO paved the way for other DAOs that were not investment vehicles – DAOs that could be agents of change.

And from the early crash and burn of The DAO, coders learned to program a safer environment where things could be decentralized once again.

New-Age Tribes

So how are we using DAOs today and what will the DAOs of the future look like?

Investment vehicle-DAOs, like the original The DAO, are still the majority but that is because blockchain was conceived for the financial realm. It was only natural that a new coin would be created and run by a DAO. The stablecoin DAI, launched by MakerDAO, has a market capitalization of US$7 billion today and is backed by real-world assets. More DAOs have followed suit, like BitDAO which invested in decentralized finance (DeFi) projects and BeetsDAO that flips NFTs, taking the concept that cryptocurrency can be crowdfunded and investments decided by the holders themselves, a step further.

However, and thankfully, that's not all that DAOs are doing today. It's not all about the money!

The ship unanimously steered by a tribe of people making decisions with the aid of an autonomous voting mechanism has sailed into uncharted territories of our lives. Today's DAOs are creating new social media ecospheres, attempting to buy the US Constitution, city planning in the metaverse, automating legal services for accessibility, decentralizing blogging, designing and marketing for Web 3.0, and advising the whole blockchain industry on governance, among other game-changing ventures. Let's look at some of them. . .

FriendsWithBenefitsDAO, or simply known as FWB, wants to see how Web 3.0 can make social media more rewarding and exclusive. Although anyone can be a member by buying tokens, what FWB is essentially doing is crowdfunding its social activities that happen in the real world – namely, New York, London, and Los Angeles, where sub-DAOs of FWB are based.

ConstitutionDAO tried to win the bid for a highly rare copy of the US Constitution auctioned by Sotheby's to preserve history and, in a rebellious decentralization fashion, stick it to the man.

A DAO created to run a game, Decentraland DAO presides over the virtual land in one of the most popular metaverse games: *Decentraland*. Players can buy and sell virtual real estate, create digital art, and play casino games, while interacting with other users. Like many virtual currencies and assets these days, the money and land in this game can fetch a pretty penny in the real world. As such, the DAO acts as both a homeowners, association and a city planning committee. Voting power is based on how much virtual property a player owns and decisions are driven toward the common goal of creating an incentivized global network of users to operate a shared virtual world.

There is a group of attorneys called LexDAO who want to make legal services more affordable, or even free. Working with programmers, they are developing blockchain projects to replace some basic and often expensive legal services.

Likewise, a group of writers are trying to use blockchain to revolutionize publishing on a platform called Mirror, which is also a DAO. Users on Mirror vote for writers in its weekly Write Race. The winners receive Write tokens, which they can exchange for publishing Mirror-hosted blogs that can be turned into NFTs. Emily Segal crowdfunded her next novel, *Burn Alpha*, using Mirror.

RaidGuild is a DAO consisting of freelance Web 3.0 builders and designers who are on a mission to fund the development of more open-source Web 3.0 tools. They do so by outsourcing their talent as a marketing and design agency for clients looking to enter the Web 3.0 world.

You can think of Uniswap DAO as the decentralized advisory committee of everything DeFi, with an aim to improve DeFi governance. Heated debates among members include a proposal to use US$40 million in the project's treasury to fund "political defense" for the broader DeFi sector.

But these are just examples of what we have today, and that is just the tip of the iceberg if we're talking about what could happen tomorrow. . .

The Monetary Authorities or Ministries of Finance of the world could be DAOs with various large financial institutions like JP Morgan, DBS, Standard Chartered, HSBC, and Citibank and more voting on new banking regulations along with large law firms like Clifford Chance and others added as members.

Government agencies giving grants could be DAOs with decisions on grant allocations being made by its members. A church could run a DAO on how offering funds are used with Deacons and senior church officials as members voting. A labor union could be a DAO with Union Members representing votes for the bigger Union Group itself. A charity could be a DAO with donors represented as members voting on how funds are used.

You could be in a neighborhood DAO voting on where a train stop should be built, which construction company should get the job, and whether to include street art on the walls.

Wouldn't you like to have a say in our future once again?

2 When the World Becomes Your Village. . .

When early humans started trading, there were obvious issues with the barter system that led to the creation of money as we know it.

Take the example of a farmer who rears chickens and wants to make a trade for a cow. If there are no cow farmers in his village, the chicken farmer would have to travel to a marketplace with all his chickens in tow and try to find a cow farmer willing to make an agreeable trade – the price has to be right for the deal to happen, 10 chickens for one cow, let's say. What if the cow farmer wants 12 chickens and all the chicken farmer has are 10 chickens, although the chicken farmer knows he'll have another 10 chickens in four months when his newly hatched chicks mature?

Wouldn't it all be easier if everyone had something portable with value and demand attached to it, that they could use to trade?

And so money was invented to get us out of the complications of barter, but it led to other problems.

Our ancestors started using rare shells to trade as that was thought to be something of stable value and in high demand at the time. In West Africa, shell money was used all the way until the mid-nineteenth century.

However, what is considered as a valuable form of currency today might be worthless tomorrow.

Gold, silver, and other precious metals were popular at various periods throughout history as they could be melted and repurposed. Both precious metals and rare shells had a wide range of uses, from ornamental to functional, but eventually the market needed something else that was more portable and could carry more value.

Finally, as we settled into the age of centralized governments, our system of currency turned into paper money, which is essentially government-guaranteed value.

But can governments really guarantee the value of our money? After printing trillions of paper notes year in and out to fund wars and relief efforts for catastrophes (some of which were ironically created by the wars), global debt surpassed US$300 trillion in 2021 according to the Institute of International Finance. This includes borrowing by governments, businesses, and households. The International Monetary Fund (IMF) warns that it is at critically high levels and that this was the biggest one-year debt surge since the World War II, brought upon by the COVID-19 pandemic.

The countries with the highest debt levels compared to GDP for 2021 were Japan (257%), Sudan (210%), Greece (207%), Eritrea (175%), and Cape Verde (161%), according to data published by Visual Capitalist.

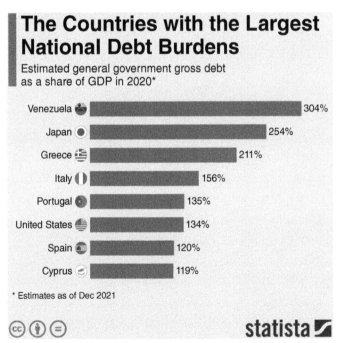

The Countries with the Largest National Debt Burdens

Estimated general government gross debt as a share of GDP in 2020*

Venezuela	304%
Japan	254%
Greece	211%
Italy	156%
Portugal	135%
United States	134%
Spain	120%
Cyprus	119%

* Estimates as of Dec 2021

statista

Historic highs

In 2020, global debt experienced the largest surge in 50 years.
(debt as a percent of GDP)

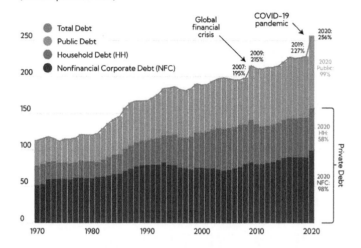

Source: With Permission of International Monetary Fund / https://
www.imf.org/en/Blogs/Articles/2021/12/15/blog-global-debt-
reaches-a-record-226-trillion

The island nation of Sri Lanka, which has over-printed
its local currency and borrowed extensively from the IMF,
recently experienced nationwide turmoil with power cuts,
internet blackouts, and fuel shortages. In 2010, US$1 was
equivalent to about 110 Sri Lankan rupees, but today that
same dollar would be worth 362 rupees. As a result of its
economic crisis, public outrage reached an all-time high in
2022. Protesters burnt down the country's president's
ancestral home, and stormed the prime minister's residence
making use of all the facilities such as the mansion's lavish
swimming pool, while some watched news reports of their
nation's leader fleeing, on the TV in his bedroom.

Now versus then

Public debt soared around the world in 2020, growing faster in some regions than during the global financial crisis.
(percent of GDP)

Public debt stock

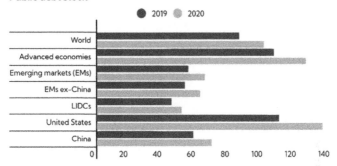

Changes in debt

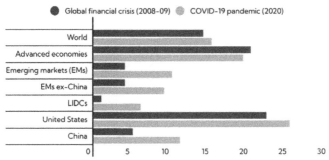

Source: With Permission of International Monetary Fund / https://www.imf.org/en/Blogs/Articles/2021/12/15/blog-global-debt-reaches-a-record-226-trillion

Similar incidents across the globe – in Greece, Turkey, and parts of South America to name a few – show just how fragile centralized leadership is and how easily a country can be thrusted into economic uncertainty. And now with the ongoing war between

▶**Sri Lanka's outstanding external debts by 2021 (in $)**

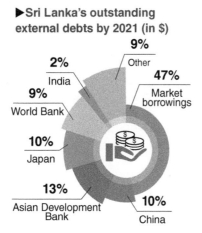

9%
Other

2%
India

47%
Market borrowings

9%
World Bank

10%
Japan

13%
Asian Development Bank

10%
China

Source: Global Times / https://www.globaltimes.cn/
page/202204/1258752.shtml last accessed December 08, 2022.

Russia and Ukraine disrupting the world's food supply, things are only going to go south for global inflation. Food prices are already soaring.

Although hyperinflation has been around since the French Revolution, the term itself describes a situation where the rate of inflation moves higher than 50% a month. In a scenario as such, local currencies would plummet. The late eighteenth century French Revolution caused France to experience its highest recorded monthly inflation – 143%.

This is nothing compared to what happened to Germany, whose monthly inflation rate reached 29 500% in 1923. Weakened economies and hungry populations are breeding grounds for corrupt politicians who rise to power through fear mongering.

Today, the United States is experiencing its highest rate of inflation in the last 40 years at 8.6%. The Consumer Price Index – the measurement of prices of a basket of goods over time – rose 7.9% in February 2022 from a year ago. The last time Americans saw prices increase this fast in a year was during the Reagan administration. The cost of inflation is adding the burden of an additional US$296 per month to average US households.

Not surprisingly, ripples are being experienced across the world, with other prosperous nations feeling the bite.

The Bank of England in June 2022 warned that inflation could reach 11% within months. Prices of goods are rising at 9.1% a year in the United Kingdom, which is coincidentally its highest rate in 40 years as well.

Triggered by a quick growth in money supply, hyperinflation happens when the warning signs are ignored.

What the United States spent amid wars in Afghanistan and Iraq post-9/11 was nothing compared to its fiscal budget today.

The Bush administration, from 2002 to 2009, increased the fiscal budget from US$2 trillion to US$3.5 trillion, spending billions a year on military solutions to combat terrorism and exert its foreign policy. What did it achieve apart from the birth of new terrorist organizations and splinter groups? Today, US national security is still on high alert for threats of terrorist attacks. Billions more is being spent on the surveillance of citizens by government agencies, with privacy-invading bills passed. And for all the time and resources spent on locating a smoking gun, they haven't found one.

President Biden's proposed fiscal budget for the United States in 2022 is US$5.8 trillion. Although it is a decrease from the US$6.8 trillion budget former President Trump submitted in 2021, this continues the trend of more US dollars being printed over the years. With ongoing conflicts that the United States is inevitably intertwined with, this is set to continue. *The New York Times* reported that the most notable spending increase was President Biden's US$773 billion military proposal – a 10% boost for the Pentagon amid concerns about the war in Ukraine and China's ambitions.

The big number here is actually US$44.8 trillion, which is how much federal debt the White House projects under Biden's plan by 2032, more than US$15 trillion above current levels according to a report by Forbes. To raise this obscene amount of money, Biden plans on taxing the richest corporations which will lead to more suffering when big businesses, especially energy companies, are unable to compete globally. In the short run, this might fix some things, but reality is every US president has tried to do this in the past and the numbers don't add up. The United States cannot survive without these corporations.

How long can the Federal Reserve keep this up? Will the United States, as a top consumer in the global economy, be able to balance its budget in the face of world inflation?

The IMF had already cut its global growth forecast to 3.6% for this year and 2023. Recession is knocking on our doors.

When We Left Gold Behind. . .

When our ancestors, like our parable farmers, had to figure out a solution to the restrictions of trade, paper money was created as a form of guarantee by central banks, and for a long time this was backed by gold as its supply-and-demand was somewhat stable.

This meant that a country could not issue more paper money than it had gold without devaluing its currency. However, the Gold Standard was too rigid. Over-mining has caused the price of gold to drop drastically throughout periods in history and, likewise, lesser demand as response to increasing prices and substitute minerals also drives the price down.

Fast forward to 1944, the United States owns two-thirds of the world's gold reserves. With the rest of the world ravaged by World War II, there was a strong need for funds to finance rebuilding. Worried that countries would start printing their own currencies exponentially, leading to another global recession, 44 nations sent delegates to a conference at Bretton Woods, New Hampshire, on 1 July 1944.

The United States, holding most of the world's gold reserves, has the most bargaining power, and ultimately all currencies ended up being linked to the US dollar, while the dollar itself was pegged to gold.

Whatever concerns the delegates of the other nations had, the conclusion was that it was the best solution everyone could agree on. The US dollar was the most obvious choice for a global currency at the time, whether other nations liked it or not. This deal made the United States the strongest nation in the world.

At the same time, the World Bank and the IMF were created to provide financial aid to less developed countries and bail out nations that were going through economic crises.

As predicted, demand for the dollar increased more than the value of the gold reserves America had. But the United States kept printing money to cover other deficits.

All of this culminated in a period of stagflation – when inflation and recession come together – in the early 1970s as the United States began to get heavily involved in the Vietnam War.

US foreign investment was causing prices to rise domestically while conversely the nation was going through economic contraction.

President Nixon began revaluing the US dollar against gold to combat stagflation. This was not enough. The United States had simply printed too much money and it was coming back to haunt the entire nation. Adding to the predicament, other nations that did not trust the United States started buying gold in large amounts, in essence, challenging America's guarantee of its currency-backed gold and its share of the real-world asset.

By 1973, Nixon completely unpegged the US dollar from gold – meaning that debts to the country could not be paid in gold and that the US dollar would be valued based on the guarantee of itself, or the US Federal Government.

The guarantee that the United States government gives is that the American economy – when its GDP, net exports, current and fiscal deficit, reserves, interest rates, and other moving parameters are taken into consideration – would hold up to its promise that a dollar will still add up to a dollar at the end of the day.

We are sitting on a crumbling system of value that will eventually end with more conflict over resources, global famine, and one or two countries controlling the value of all the currencies of the world.

It is obvious that a new system of trade must emerge, and it must not be connected to traditional currencies. We need to redefine what value really is.

Are 10 chickens really worth one cow and can we apply this to an exchange of services? Does the chicken farmer need to wait for his new hatchlings to mature to sell them? What if we could turn the whole world into a virtual marketplace with efficient systems of verification, smart contracts, logistics, and e-commerce powered by Web 3.0 technology?

The world would truly be your village then.

The Corruption of Trade

Traditional systems of trade have been long corrupted. "Free trade" is only practiced between countries that are friendly with each other and guess what – many countries don't get along with each other.

Hence, governments place sanctions, tariffs, quotas, and other barriers on international trade or explicitly prohibit trading activities with countries they are not friendly with, while giving trade subsidies to those that can return the favor in one form or another – for example providing them with military protection.

Add in an inflated currency market dominated by the US dollar, and you've now got a world where crude oil can only be bought in greenbacks.

The petrodollar system was introduced in the early 1970s after the Bretton Woods Gold Standard ended. This essentially gave the United States, which had entered into an agreement with Saudi Arabia to standardize oil sales in US dollars, an obviously unfair advantage to the rest of the world's currencies.

With the United States' foreign policy of treading into places where they are unwanted, and the massive fall of its banking, automotive, and farming industries to name a few that have been bailed out by Congress, it is alarming what is in store for the world based on one government's decision-making skills or lack of.

Trade is no longer associated with one's free will to seek livelihood. Trade is now a weapon of governments.

But what if we could change this with Web 3.0 and blockchain?

If the whole world was connected as a marketplace with large and small traders alike offering every item imaginable up for sale or trade, with a trustable system of payment and verification encrypted into smart contracts, would we be able to bypass the draconian rules imposed upon our current trade system?

Imagine cutting out interference by inefficient, biased government bodies. Would free trade really live up to its name then?

Decentralized Trading, Reputation Tokens, and the Death of the Irresponsible Influencer-Marketer

Today, if an American farmer wanted to list his chickens as commodities, he would have to go to the Chicago Mercantile Exchange (CME) – a government-regulated exchange that decides what can get listed as a Futures contract.

Essentially what the CME does is turn physical assets into paper value, giving it portability so people can trade on the future value of those assets. There is a lengthy and questionable process of verification of assets, and not every American farmer would qualify to have their livestock listed.

In a world driven by Web 3.0 innovation, bodies like the CME would be rendered useless. Bypassing government middlemen, transparency would not be an issue as smart contracts, driven by blockchain technology, Web 3.0, and the Internet of Things will enable verification while active Decentralized Autonomous Organizations (DAOs) would police the behavior and conduct of traders through so-called reputation tokens.

Barter 2.0 is how I would describe this new, brave global marketplace.

Small traders would be able to enter this marketplace with just an internet connection and their smartphones, and list their businesses on a global scale. In African nations, where conflict and government sanctions have disrupted traditional marketplaces and the import and export of goods, this is already being done.

By digitizing their inventory, traders can use it as collateral to take out stablecoin loans and scale their businesses. Now, the dilemma of the farmer who has two chickens short for a trade is no longer a problem.

Any product that a trader wants to sell or trade, as long as it can be verified by the technology available which is bound to leap in improvement in the future, can be tokenized into a digital asset. Farmers will no longer have to wait for their crops to grow to sell them. By tokenizing their projections, they will be able to work out smart contracts with buyers or make trades with others, and cash out immediately upon a successful deal.

Reputation tokens (RTs) will play a huge role as indicators of how trustworthy a trader is beyond the verification technology of the day. Using these tokens, DAOs will emerge to take care of certain aspects of policing the communities found on Barter 2.0. In a simple scenario that mirrors penalty cards in soccer – red RTs could be given for serious offenses, whereby the DAO might ban the trader from the platform. Conversely green RTs could be awarded for good behavior between traders, and orange RTs could be the warnings a trader would get before being banned.

Think of RTs as a decentralized credit score for decentralized societies. Now a customer's opinion does matter. Government regulations are fallible and guilty traders often walk away with a fine equivalent to a drop in the sea by the standards of their wealth. Think of celebrities or influencers who become so-called entrepreneurs by cashing in on their fame by selling questionable products (let's say slimming products containing banned substances that give adverse side effects – believe it or not, this is a legit, booming homegrown industry in Malaysia driven by influencer marketing, which is causing a looming healthcare crisis).

Just because something has a lot of likes on Facebook doesn't mean it's good for you. The social media giant's algorithms will amplify posts with bad behavior due to the reactions and engagements they receive. This leads to a cycle of stupidity and conniving schemes as people follow them and amplify their messages that could have been stopped with DAOs and RTs removing credibility from those who influence via bad behavior.

The sooner we kill influencer marketing that is based on irresponsible behavior, the sooner the world will progress.

Can't Buy Me Love. . .

Aside from the benefits of having portability for trade, money is essentially useless. It is value printed on notes that is guaranteed by governments in a world where governments are crumbling.

In a Barter 2.0 economy, there will be an evolution in the trade of value. The current generation entering today's workforce (Gen Z) are already adopting and bringing humanity toward a digital economy. Safe to say, we have moved past the era of Internet of Data and are in the era of Internet of Money right now, and it will continue to evolve.

Cryptocurrency and centralized bank digital currencies (CBDCs) will be the staple currencies in 5–10 years. Governments, no matter how much they resist it, will eventually want to be a part of this new world – a world that we could build based on the theoretical concepts of what could be done with Web 3.0 architecture. Whichever government that manages to integrate this tech into their existing processes will be the first to reap the benefits and stay ahead of the rest.

Ahead of this curve, we will see a leap where humans will no longer trade with money and assets but with their skills or passion.

Value doesn't stay in a monetary system, and we already knew this. As mentioned, primitive humans used to trade with rare shells, gold, and other metals as currency until banks were created and with it, paper money. But there was another way of trading that most historians and anthropologists would agree was common among ancient tribes. It was the exchange of value via a good deed.

Tribe members did not calculate the value of objects, tools, meals, or trophies, but looked upon them as good deeds. After all, they were already sharing their food supply as hunters and gatherers.

Gifting a necklace to a neighbor, for example, could be returned in favor by a good deed like caring for them when they are ill. Strangely, or naturally, since these tribes were small, close knitted societies, the practice of "paying it forward," whereby a tribe member would respond to a person's kindness by being kind to someone else in the tribe, was also commonplace.

With new layers of value that Barter 2.0 can bring that are currently not in the global GDP, humans might very well just move past money as value and move back to the ancient practice of paying it forward, where value is not derived from cash.

How would this work when we are no longer small groups of people trying to survive in the wilderness? When we have bills and utilities to pay? When there is a global economy based on supply and demand?

The answer is in variety. Anything can be monetized as long as there are willing buyers or fulfilling trades. This includes the service and creative industry and our time. A lawyer might provide legal counsel in exchange for housekeeping services, a doctor could treat an artist who would pay with NFT art, good Samaritans could be rewarded for community work with RTs.

Humanity has gone from the exchange of value (barter) to the store of value (gold) to the invention of currency (paper money) and now we're moving back to the exchange of value through meaningful actions. This is the future we hope to create, and it will be a colorful future too.

Skills and services are at the core of what we as humans can provide so we can expect a flourishing of the gig economy. As most humans are multi-talented, everyone will have more than one source of income.

If we could all find a fulfilling trade in exchange for our skills and services, the world would have long been done with the concept of money. But alas, certain groups of the elite keep us where we are because they set the rules. Nowhere is this more evident than the content creation industry which is now dominated, and will be dominated for the near future, by on-demand streaming companies that took over the role that traditional Hollywood and music labels played before the age of Web 2.0 internet.

In terms of content creation and media, individuality will drive future products and services as creators compete on a global scale. A new creator economy will be born as blockchain storage becomes more robust. Enjoying full feature films and music albums bought on the blockchain will be possible – tying ownership to the creator or artist, ensuring a proper flow of royalties, and disrupting streaming giants like Netflix and Spotify. Content creators would be able to host their own creations on the blockchains and cut out the middleman.

A Barter 2.0 economy will eventually lead to the digitization or tokenization of everything under the sky – all assets including skillsets and potential worth of assets (futures). There wouldn't be anything from the real world that you couldn't buy on the Web 3.0 market which would be open 24 hours a day, seven days a week.

Surely, we can all see the value in that.

3 The New Centralization

The flow of money and creation of new money for a nation are governed by its Central Bank. In times of crisis, central banks can either save or destroy the economy with good or bad policies.

Central banks are established to conduct the monetary policy and control the money supply of nations. On a macro-scale, they do this by adjusting interest rates and facilitating operations on the open market, taking charge of the flow of cash in the economy and loans of the nation.

Central banks also work on a micro-scale by setting the reserve ratio of commercial banks, meaning they set the percentage of deposits a commercial bank is required to keep as cash. Once a commercial bank's reserves dips below this level, they may turn to their central bank to bail them out.

As mentioned in the previous chapter, money is not printed out of thin air – it is supposed to be backed by the economic growth and prospects of a nation, after we left behind the Gold Standard. Thus, increasing a nation's money supply by releasing new cash into the economy must be guided by an independent entity that is free from the influence of the ruling regime.

Mandated with keeping a low, predictable inflation rate and steady GDP growth, central banks can effectively reject and amend the government's fiscal budget if it is bloated or favors corporate profit over the public's interest.

We can think of central banks as the government's bank. As currency is backed by a government's promise of a better tomorrow, central banks have the duty of being a reality check on government spending. Printing more money will lead to more inflation; however, the justification is that printing more money is needed to stimulate GDP growth, which creates more jobs as the economy grows. Therefore, it is crucial that central banks ensure the government spends the money wisely and does not print it in excess as if it comes out of thin air.

In 1668, Sweden's parliament founded the Riksens Ständers Bank (the Estates of the Realm Bank), arguably one of the world's oldest central banks, to regulate commercial banks and the nation's economy. Almost three centuries later in 1913, the Federal Reserve System – the central banking system of the

United States – was created after a series of financial panics led to the need for central control of the nation's monetary system.

After World War II, at the Bretton Woods conference, the world decided to use the US dollar as the global trading currency as the United States owned the majority of the world's gold reserves. However, when President Nixon decided to unpeg the US dollar from gold, the boundaries that limited the printing of the US dollar were somewhat removed.

One of the chief criticisms of the Gold Standard that caused its demise was that the supply of newly minted gold was not flexible enough to keep up with the growing global economy. A country might not be able to keep up with inflation as well, like following World War II, when additional loans were needed chiefly by Europe and Asia, where war had ravaged whole cities and economies, and other nations across the seas that were affected by proxy as the colonies of Western powers that depended on the Western economy.

By unpegging gold, Nixon gave the Federal Reserve (Fed) and the US government more power to steer the global economy by printing the currency the world trades in, the US dollar, without the restrictions of the Gold Standard. The US dollar is now worth what the US government says it is worth based on its GDP and other movable parameters of the economy.

Although the Gold Standard had its weak points, paper money was linked to a physical asset that could control inflation by limiting the supply of money printed, and there would be a tangible cap to how much a government could print before risking accelerated inflation.

With the responsibility of being the sole regulator of the world's trading currency, the Fed needs to be run independently from the influence of the US government.

Due to its complexities, many conspiracy theories have arisen on who is really behind the Fed. However, finding out the truth might just be digging a deeper hole. . .

Who Owns the Fed?

Since the Civil War, the US economy had gone through several periods of depression after nationwide panics led people to withdraw their money all at once. Commercial banks weren't backed by a central bank, so no one could save them if they went bust. Due to this, rumors of insolvency ruined and bankrupted otherwise healthy banks.

It was obvious that a central bank was needed to unite the banks in the country and bail them out if needed but that was the only thing everyone could agree on.

After Congress passed legislation to create a central bank, it took another five years of heated debates and negotiations for a conclusion to be reached. Bankers were concerned about interference from politicians and wanted it to be as independent as possible from Washington. Meanwhile, the government, needing funds for its fiscal budget and foreign policy spending, did not exactly trust the bankers as well.

Gathering on a resort on Jekyll Island in Georgia, hundreds of miles away from Capitol Hill, an elite club of the wealthiest American bankers, industrialists, and businessmen led by John Morgan conceived the idea of what America's first central bank would look like, and it was unlikely any power structure that any central bank had seen. Finally, in 1913, the Federal Reserve was born.

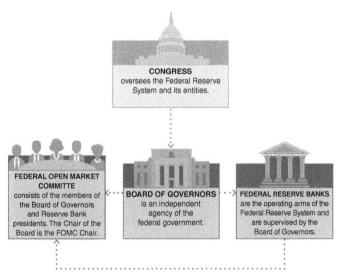

Source: Board of Governors

Devised so that policymakers could hear from all sides, including the American public, the Federal Reserve System, or the Fed, is governed by the Federal Reserve Board of Governors, regional reserve banks, and the Federal Open Market Committee (FOMC). The Federal Reserve Bank is made of 12 regional reserve banks governed by local bankers and businessmen.

Although the Fed is not owned by anyone, it works with the government via the Board of Governors in Washington D.C., an agency of the federal government that reports to and is directly accountable to Congress.

The Board, which comprises seven governors, is appointed by the president and confirmed by the Senate. The seven governors make up the voting majority in the FOMC, with the remaining five votes coming from regional reserve bank presidents.

The FOMC sets monetary policy for the United States. Among its current tasks is a long-run inflation target of 2%.

To limit the president's power, they can only appoint one governor of the Board every two years with a 14-year term. The Board provides general guidance for the Federal Reserve System and oversees the 12 regional reserve banks, which serve as bankers for commercial banks in their regions. Each of the 12 reserve banks of the Federal Reserve System is owned by its member banks, who originally gave capital in exchange for shares in these reserve banks.

Testifying before Congress, the Board submits the Monetary Policy Report on recent economic developments and their plans for monetary policy twice a year. Independently audited financial statements of the System are disclosed publicly, as are the minutes from FOMC meetings.

Every bank in America is required by law to keep 6% of its capital in its regional reserve bank. Their capital is exchanged for shares which cannot be sold. Instead, these shares give the shareholder the right to vote on about two-thirds of the Board of Directors of their regional reserve bank. Larger banks will have larger surpluses of capital and naturally more shares and influence.

So who owns the Fed? Basically, every big bank in America. The full list is 150 pages long, but a few names stand out.

With Wall Street under its jurisdiction, the New York Fed is the most important regional reserve bank and component of the Federal Reserve Bank's network in America. Apart from open market operations, the New York Fed conducts transactions in foreign exchange markets for the Federal Reserve System and US Treasury. Due to this, the New York Fed president, who also serves as FOMC vice chair, is the only regional reserve bank president who serves as a permanent voting member of the FOMC.

Take a guess how many commercial banks own the majority of shares in the New York Fed?

The answer is just two – Citibank holds 42.8% of shares, while JP Morgan has 29.5% of the total. This majority percentage of ownership held by these two giants has not changed much since 2007, when JP Morgan owned 41.7% and Citibank had 36.6%.

To quote George Selgin, director of the Center for Monetary and Financial Alternatives at the Cato Institute in Washington D.C., in a report by Institutional Investor, "The Fed is facing a difficult challenge. It's trying to become more transparent while its operations become more complex. That's a difficult trick to pull off."

The Fed was created for the American public, to bring stability, but has it been creating more inflation and distress globally?

To Teach the World to Sing in Perfect Harmony

Almost every nation in the world today uses a central bank to make their monetary policies. The handful of countries that don't have central banks are island nations with low populations that mostly trade with the US dollar and euro.

Central banks often purchase assets to help back their financial system. As of 2016, approximately 75% of the world's central bank assets are held by China, the United States, Japan, and some European countries.

It can be said that the whole world now operates on a centralized monetary system that revolves around the United States and its allies. But is the situation really that bad, with the International Monetary Fund (IMF) acting as regulator and the World Bank bailing out countries that have fallen into poverty?

An excerpt taken from the book *US Relations with the World Bank, 1945–1992* by Catherine Gwin reads: "Throughout the history of the International Bank for Reconstruction and Development (the World Bank), the United States has been the largest shareholder and the most influential member country. US support for, pressure on, and criticisms of the Bank have been central to its growth and the evolution of its policies, programs, and practices."

Working as if they are instruments of the US government and its allies, the World Bank and IMF have, for borrowings, subjugated nations in the past and supported dictatorships that violated international pacts on human rights. On the other hand, the US government can pressure these financial institutions to impose trade tariffs or stop giving loans to certain ruling parties – such as when it refused to grant loans

to France due to the French Communist Party (PCF)
being in the government, post-World War II.

Gwin elaborates the relationship of the United
States and the World Bank in these excerpts taken from
her book, *The World Bank, Its First Half Century,
Volume 2*:

> The top management of the [World] Bank spends
> much more time meeting with, consulting, and
> responding to the United States than it does with
> any other member country. Although this intense
> interaction has changed little over the years, the way
> the United States mobilizes other member countries
> in support of its views has changed considerably.
> Initially, it was so predominant that its positions
> and the decision of the board were virtually
> indistinguishable.

Going as far as to state that "The United States has
viewed all multilateral organizations, including the
World Bank, as instruments of foreign policy to be
used for specific US aims and objectives" and "is often
impatient with the processes of consensus building on
which multilateral cooperation rests," the book rips
apart any preconceived notion of justice that the US
government should hold as regulators of the world's
financial institutions.

The book entails how the relationship between the
United States and the World Bank changed over the
years: "A preoccupation with containing communism,

and the change in the relative US power in the world explain much of the evolution in US relations with the World Bank over the past fifty years," adding that, "The debt crisis in the south and the collapse of communism in eastern Europe led to renewed US interest in the Bank."

It may look as if the financial system we have now is the best we can ask for under the circumstances; however, things are going to get even more centralized as the world embraces digital currency.

Central Bank Digital Currencies and Data Collection

If cryptocurrency is meant to liberalize finance, as we've seen happening within the decentralized finance (DeFi) movement, then Central Bank Digital Currencies (CBDCs) conversely are meant to bring us closer centralization and give central banks more power than anyone has seen before in the history of finance. Blockchain got rid of the middleman, but CBDCs will inevitably give the middleman access to all our financial data. We are about to begin a new age of unrelentless financial surveillance and control.

While CBDCs will make criminal activities like money laundering more difficult, what is pushing this new digital currency forward is the promise of GDP growth as a result of faster transactions. Some financial institutions like the Bank of England (the UK's central bank) thinks it can be bullish against inflation, while others speak of the pooled liquidity that will benefit nations that adopt a CBDC.

However, what we will be giving up is whatever that is left of our financial privacy. A CBDC is reportable, unchangeable, traceable, and accessible to anyone with an internet connection. There will be no dodging taxes as all your income and expenses will be viewable at the click of a button.

Digital currency controlled by central banks will no doubt bring us closer to a Big Brother scenario, where every digital wallet will contain information that will be pulled into a database for governments to analyze and even be given credit scores, just like how banks use your information to fulfill Know Your Customer guidelines to identify suitability and risks involved in a business relationship.

Secrecy laws might still exist in this future, but how far will the law go to protect someone who is incriminated by government agencies? Currently, most nations' laws require a court order for government agencies to investigate financial data. In the future, governments will no longer require court orders as they will have full access to your data.

From creating financial policies to controlling the entire transaction highway of an economy, there is much public fear regarding the limitless power that we are handing over to our governments.

Just like crypto, CBDCs will run on the blockchain.

Part of the rationale behind governments allowing cryptocurrencies to operate and trade within their nations in the past decade is that they needed to see the experiment live. A nationwide switch from paper money to digital money would not have been possible before the emergence of cryptocurrency as it would have been too much of a shock for the public.

Considering cybersecurity at the time, hacking was a concern as there was no network of computers doing verifications with distributed ledger technology as we have now with blockchain. A single hack could destabilize a whole nation's economy if CBDCs had been introduced in the past.

Today's world is far more tech-savvy. We have non-fungible tokens (NFTs), gaming currencies, and other forms of digital value with liquidity that are commonly traded. A change from paper money to CBDCs will be almost effortlessly supported by the public.

Is Anything Real Anymore?

We would appear alien to our ancient ancestors who carried out trading activities with rare shells and minerals, but just 20 years ago, it would have been hard to explain the concept of digital currency to the man on the street.

It is likely that we will see CBDCs take over world trade in the coming years; some countries like China have already started.

However, CBDCs still function like paper money at the end of the day, with all its shortcomings. Not being backed by real-world assets, a CBDC is still fiat currency tied in value to the government's promise.

The irony now is that Web 3.0 tools meant to bring freedom and level the field are being turned against us by the same people who we entrusted to keep the economy safe. And the more the public catches on to what is happening with the global financial system, the more distrust arises. Hence, there is consensus that the value of money is only safe when we convert it into something tangible with utility, like land or stocks. However, even these assets can be inflated and can crash when the market panics.

Standing as an intermediary currency are stablecoins. Backed by real-world assets, stablecoins are cryptocurrencies designed to be protected from the volatility that challenges the use of crypto for payments or as a store of value.

Stablecoins are the antithesis to the hype around crypto investors' wild gains and losses as they attempt to maintain a constant exchange rate with fiat currencies.

Much like how commercial banks operate, centralized stablecoins like Tether (USDT), USD Coin (USDC), and Zytara USD (ZUSD) make money through lending and investing. This is done by fractional reserve banking where only a fraction of deposits are required to be backed by physical cash that can be withdrawn by investors at any given time.

All three of these stablecoins are pegged to the US dollar and redeemable on a 1:1 basis.

Backed "100% by Tether's reserves," as stated on its website, Tether is owned by iFinex, a Hong Kong-registered company that also owns crypto exchange BitFinex. Most of Tether's reserves are cash and common cash equivalents. In their latest assurance opinion, Tether revealed that over 55% of their reserves are now US Treasuries and that commercial paper now makes up less than 29% of their vault. Tether helps investors move funds between cryptocurrency markets and the traditional financial system.

USDC, on the other hand, only holds cash and short-term US government bonds, according to its monthly report. Its reserves are held in the custody and management of US financial institutions, including BlackRock and BNY Mellon. Conceived by CENTRE, an open-source fintech project funded by contributions from Circle and Coinbase, USDC is governed by this organization whose goal is to connect the public and all merchants, financial institutions, and currencies across the globe into one independent and stable financial system.

With aspirations to make cryptocurrency more user-friendly, USDC was developed to be used by smaller businesses and individuals as well, not just big corporations. USDC provides an open-source smart contract, allowing companies to create and develop their own blockchain products like wallets and exchanges.

Built on Ethereum Blockchain, ZUSD is a digital currency that can be easily sent and received like email. Issued by a regulated financial institution, each ZUSD is redeemable through Prime Trust at a 1:1 ratio to the US dollar and subject to audits by an independent accounting firm, with reports made publicly available on a regular basis.

Designed for the future of finance, esports, gaming, and a host of other applications, ZUSD and other blockchain-based assets seek to enable financial connectivity within this global community, solving the industry's many pain points with transactions while simultaneously promoting financial inclusion and literacy.

Since the fall of TerraUSD (UST) in mid-2022, the US government has come down hard with a legal framework around how stablecoins should operate.

A newly introduced bill by the US Congress will set requirements for the amount of backing assets stablecoin issuers are required to hold, among other things. The latest regulator to step in is the New York State Department of Financial Services (DFS), which made a public guidance on the issuance of stablecoins backed by US dollars.

Although some are preoccupied with the market news of UST, with these new checks put in place by regulating agencies, US dollar backed stablecoins look more promising as an alternative for transactions and put some distance between your financial information and the government.

What stablecoins promise, apart from stability and acting as a go-between for digital and fiat currencies, is that there will always be other options to CBDCs as we move forward in a world that is not only getting smaller but also less private.

You Can't Always Get What You Want. . .

Decentralization, security, and scalability are three variables that persistently strive to function in harmony so that DeFi can work for the world at large. But in reality, these factors work against each other in their designs.

The "Blockchain Trilemma" is a term used to conceptualize the tricky act of enforcing each of these

variables without compromising or diminishing the
strength of the other. People often use the analogy of
balancing your work life with play and sleep, or even
the infamous conundrum of the service industry where
clients want everything delivered fast, cheap, and
with quality.

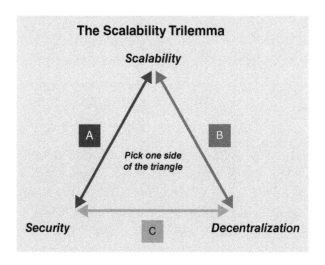

Source: Medium Michael Zochowski / https://medium.com/
logos-network/everything-you-know-about-the-scalability-
trilemma-is-probably-wrong-bc4f4b7a7ef

    The first variable, decentralization, is the act of
distributing power in a bid to be free of central
authority. In terms of blockchain, we have individual
nodes (a network of supercomputers around the world)
powering the system. The more nodes we have, the
more decentralized the blockchain becomes, which is
the whole purpose of decentralization. However, the

time it takes to process transactions increases as more nodes take more time to come to a consensus to authenticate a transfer.

Scalability is affected because we have to wait for the entire network to collectively agree, although decentralized and secure, it is also inefficient if compared to transactions validated by a single entity. Visa can process as many as 1700 TPS (transactions per second), while Bitcoin is capable of only processing up to 5 TPS.

Blockchains that use Proof-of-Work (PoW) mechanisms, where computers consume energy in a race to randomly create a unique hash in a bid to process the transaction, are secured in a sense that a hacker needs to take control of over 51% of the network to manipulate the results. They are, however, not scalable and, thus, not entirely practical for the everyday citizen.

Ethereum's move to a Proof-of-Stake (PoS) mechanism, where nodes do not have to solve complex mathematical equations but instead require validators to stake a certain amount of crypto as collateral, can be seen as a step forward in solving the Blockchain Trilemma and also furthering blockchain's goal of decentralization.

As only validators that can afford to put up the collateral can have a stake in processing transactions, fewer nodes will qualify, hence, reducing the time it takes and increasing scalability. Ethereum 2.0 will reportedly be able to handle up to 100 000 TPS, dwarfing Visa's processing power several 100-fold. Security is also tightened in PoS, as a hacker would require 51% of the total staked cryptocurrencies to initiate a hijack.

PoS' weakness is its compromise, decentralization. With the power to validate transactions in the hands of a few, many argue that this defeats the purpose of decentralization.

Developers have been cracking their heads for more than a decade trying to figure out a way for all three variables that make the Blockchain Trilemma to be addressed. Many blockchain companies have implemented Layer 1 and Layer 2 changes to their systems in an effort to create the perfect system of consensus that can be safely adopted by everyone.

The Algorand blockchain, for example, is attempting to make PoS more decentralized by randomizing the selection of validators.

Tackling scalability, blockchains like Zilliqa and Ethereum 2.0, is using a technology known as "sharding," where groups of transactions are broken down into "shards" and then processed in parallel by the network, speeding up the process by allowing nodes to validate transactions in batches.

Layer 2 solutions complement and exist as a separate layer on top of the foundation of the blockchain. These are upgrades that do not necessarily solve the Trilemma, but help to make existing processes more efficient. For example, Bitcoin has introduced a Layer 2 upgrade known as the Lightning Network which enables the crypto-pioneer to handle more transactions, improving the main weakness in Bitcoin's current form: scalability.

Among the most exciting developments is the potential for blockchains to work together. There are currently more than 20 000 blockchain companies in the world and they do not have interoperability. This means they pretty much exist in their own bubbles with few to no avenues of communication between each other.

If blockchains could unite, they could capitalize on each other's strengths and complement solutions to their weaknesses. Chains could operate independently in governance, the same way they are doing now, but team up to bring the world closer to mass decentralization.

The idea of interoperability is championed by many within the DeFi movement. Notably, Polkadot is a protocol trying to achieve blockchain cooperation with a "relay chain" integrated into its core programming for higher scalability. Designed to support multiple chains on a single network, Polkadot uses "parachains," which are independent blockchains connected to the main relay chain. The chains that reside on Polkadot's network will gain paramount added security but still operate independently.

An evolved PoS concept is used in Polkadot's validating mechanism. Nominated Proof of Stake (NPoS) is different from PoS in that NPoS has validators and nominators who are both rewarded for their role in decentralization and security.

The validators are actual nodes that stake DOT (Polkadot's native token) tokens to assess transactions on the Relay Chain, while the nominators who do not have to put in a stake help to secure the Relay Chain by nominating trustworthy validators. It is like having two sets of validation instead of one – for the transaction itself and another for the validator.

Without developers truckin' on in the face of the Trilemma, the blockchain industry would not have been able to progress to the level it is at now. The future will see the integration of more blockchain platforms as the community realizes that cooperation and consensus are needed to overcome fundamental problems and create the bankless world of the future that we all desire to witness someday.

4 Tower of Babel 2.0

About 90 kilometers south of Baghdad, under the scorching heat of the Iraqi sun, more than 200 workers toiled daily, year-round for 15 years from 1899 to 1914, to excavate the ruins of ancient Babylon.

Led by German archeologist Robert Koldewey, the site that had been identified a century earlier by British assyriologist Claudius James Rich bore fruitful discoveries right from the start of the expedition. In the first year alone, remnants of Babylon's central Processional Street were unearthed, giving the modern world its first look at the "City of Cities" which vanished off the face of the earth, either swallowed by the desert or destroyed in repeated invasions.

Subsequent discoveries marveled the world further with the Hanging Gardens of Babylon and palaces of King Nebuchadnezzar uncovered, fueling a resurgence in the interest of biblical scholarship as well as the studies of various religions that have historical reference to the city of Babylon and its rulers.

The discovery by Robert Koldewey that linked all variations of folklore, religions, and documented accounts of Babylon, however, was Etemenanki. With the remains of its foundation, and outer and inner walls visible from aerial view, the sprawling building was a temple ziggurat dedicated to the Babylonian god Marduk.

Although many Christians in the world today believe Etemenanki to be the biblical Tower of Babel, Koldeway's findings not only gave plausibility to this theory but also opened more possibilities to how the fable of this ancient-world wonder continued to influence cultures and religions around the globe long after its destruction.

Meaning "temple of the foundation of heaven and earth" in ancient Sumerian, Etemenanki's remains are now kept as part of the Schøyen Collection. Among the rumble of artifacts preserved by the private Norwegian collection is Etemenanki's stele – a black ceremonial stone used as a plaque to inscribe the official notes or message of the ruler on the structure's construction.

The translation of the royal declaration of King Nebuchadnezzar II found on the plaque notes that the ruler "mobilized all countries" and "each and every ruler" for its construction:

ETEMENANKI: ZIKKURAT BABIBLI: "THE HOUSE, THE FOUNDATION OF HEAVEN AND EARTH, ZIGGURAT IN BABYLON."

NEBUCHADNEZZAR, KING OF
BABYLON AM I – IN ORDER TO COMPLETE
E-TEMEN-ANKI AND E-UR-ME-IMIN-
ANKI I MOBILIZED ALL COUNTRIES
EVERYWHERE, EACH AND EVERY RULER
WHO HAD BEEN RAISED TO PROMINENCE
OVER ALL THE PEOPLE OF THE WORLD –
LOVED BY MARDUK, FROM THE UPPER
SEA TO THE LOWER SEA, THE DISTANT
NATIONS, THE TEEMING PEOPLE OF THE
WORLD, KINGS OF REMOTE MOUNTAINS
AND FAR-FLUNG ISLANDS... I COMPLETED
IT RAISING ITS TOP TO THE HEAVEN,
MAKING IT GLEAM BRIGHT AS THE SUN
— *Robert Koldewey /*
Wikimedia Commons / Public Domain

Source: Robert Koldewey / Wikimedia Commons / Public Domain

Source: Robert Koldewey / Wikimedia Commons / Public Domain

It is unknown when Etemenanki was originally constructed but historians agree that it had been destroyed and rebuilt several times over centuries by generations of rulers.

Suffice to say, with many nomadic tribes passing by, and some settling in Babylon, various versions of Etemenanki's origin exist in numerous sacred scriptures, from the religions in proximity like Christianity, Judaism, and Islam to even religions in faraway lands like Hinduism (in India and Nepal), and the religions of the Karen of Myanmar, the Tohono O'odham people of Arizona, and the people of Botswana and Polynesia.

A majority of these accounts and versions of Etemenanki are popularly associated with man's desire to reach the heavens, or to achieve a level of power equal to that of God.

In Christianity and Judaism, the Tower of Babel is widely accepted as an allegorical tale of men's hubris and fall in defying God, and an origin myth explaining the world's languages.

In the Bible, the Tower of Babel is one of the events that took place after the great flood in which Noah and his descendants survived. Genesis 11:1–9 tells its story and gives the explanation of the existence of diverse human languages.

In this first chapter of the Bible, the Babylonians wanting to make a name for themselves collectively decided to construct a mighty city and a structure "with its top in the heavens." Scholars have noted that the Babylonians were also trying to escape God's wrath should he send another flood to reset the world.

Seeing their unrelenting progress, God was not pleased and disrupted their work by making them speak different tongues. Because the workers couldn't understand each other's languages, they could work not together. Confusion arose. Consensus broke.

Babylon, the great city that archeologists discovered in the last century, came later. In this first attempt, which in Jewish scripture (the Antiquities of the Jews) says is spearheaded by King Nimrod, the great grandson of Noah, the city and tower were never completed, and the people were eventually scattered around the world. Speaking different languages, they would never be able to attempt the same feat.

In Islam, a similar tale is told, however, in a different location. Pharaoh tried to reach the God of Moses to challenge Him and call Him a liar.

Muslims believe that God created nations to know each other and not to be separated; hence, the idea of the Tower of Babel is non-compliant to Islamic belief, but the story told in the Quran suggests that Pharaoh tried to achieve something similar as what the Babylonians strived for albeit with a different motive, and succeeded in constructing a significant portion, before God responded by halting progress as he did with the Babylonians.

Interestingly, sizable monolithic ruins found in other parts of the world suggest that the Etemenanki might not be the only one of its kind.

Lost in Translation

We often imagine the ancient world based on remnants of what we can see today. There is a large part of the picture that is left to be found. With wars that have devastated cities like Babylon, it is plausible that the world's first skyscrapers were temples and portals intended to reach the heavens.

Similar adaptations of this story are told in other religions, some differing more than others but the central themes of men challenging God or wanting to reach God the wrong way, and the ability to create a monumental structure with consensus, are prevalent.

From a non-religious point of view, the destruction of the tower was most likely due to unsustainability and over-development brought by consensus to achieve a large-scale project that served no purpose but fulfill a certain image of progress, much like the GDP rating for any country under a corrupt government today.

However, progressing faster than the environment and financial ecosystem can cope with is not the only reason why a construction project could fail. Any good project leader knows when to issue a stop-work order before a catastrophe happens or at least address an issue at grassroots level before it becomes a major incident. There must be another human factor leading to the tower's fall, and it can't be due to things lost in translation.

The difference in languages is often the scapegoat for miscommunication and even for opposing the unity of humanity. But language is fluid – the English language alone contains thousands of words from other languages, and the same goes for other languages of the world. Humans have been integrating long before Babel.

Whichever version of tale of the Tower of Babel we choose to dissect there is one similarity – that consensus propels a group of people forward; the fact that people are speaking the same tongue only makes the goal easier to be understood. The reconstruction of the tower could have very well continued if the builders had managed to move past language barriers and came back to their consensus, which if one believes Etemenanki to be the fabled Tower of Babel, then this is evidently what happened later.

Etemenanki, rebuilt under different kings, reaching the skies again and again, making builders richer and more boisterous, selfish, and arrogant with every cycle of construction, would have been doomed to have a broken consensus each time before God had to revisit his own wrath.

Without consensus, a goal is no more than someone else's desire. No work could possibly start without an agreement made by all parties involved. Conversely, the sky is the limit when total consensus of the population is reached.

The Babylonian Empire, and with it, Etemenanki, finally fell for the last time in 593 BC, when the city was conquered by Persian king Cyrus the Great. Fittingly, in the aftermath, the residents of Babylon plundered the Tower of Babel and used its bricks to build their own houses.

The Language of Progress

Our world is defined by the language we speak and think in. How far our imaginations can stretch is only limited by the words in which we can express our ideas, and, in parallel, how much our world changes is dependent on how we interact with it, including what words we choose to use in our daily conversations.

Considered by some to be the greatest philosopher of the twentieth century, Ludwig Wittgenstein's works were rigorously rejected by the academicians of his time. The Austrian–British philosopher of logic, mathematics, the mind, and language said, "The limits of my language mean the limits of my world."

Wittgenstein wrote only one book during his entire life, *Tractatus Logico-Philosophicus* (Logical-Philosophical Treatise). He began formulating the core ideas around his book while serving as a soldier in the trenches of World War I, scribbling notes under mortar bombardments before his military leave in the summer of 1918.

In *Tractatus Logico-Philosophicus*, the author challenges how we think of language and logic, or, at least, how people thought of it up until the early 1900s. Wittgenstein states that the primary function of language is to allow us to visually picture the abstract, and not just reality. This purpose is known as picture theory and it was a building block in the Logical Positivism school of thought that defined modern philosophy until the 1960s.

Up until this point, the standard and pursuit of philosophy was mostly kept by and for the rich, as like quality education today is mostly reserved for the elite who can make donations to Ivy League universities. On the subject of language, the common philosophical belief at the time was that language mirrored reality. It was a means to an end, a tool used to describe what the world was. A one-way road of information – perception of reality goes into our minds and words come out.

Wittgenstein believed that language was more powerful than this and that it could shape the world. He asserted that language is used as a description of the logical form of reality, and not reality itself. Propositions or philosophical opinions are as such logical pictures of what we perceive to be our reality. It is a picture of reality and not reality itself. Language is fluid and ever evolving as we interact with our world, and the words we choose to use or invent to describe something, evidently affects our surroundings as well. In his own words, Wittgenstein suggests that it isn't what we say that matters, rather it is the way that we say it and the context in which we say it that counts, or as he puts it, "Words are how you use them."

The way we use language also shapes reality. We can see this when certain societies progress past racism – with some societies banning derogatory terms from being used freely and making them punishable by law if said publicly. We see it over generations with mothers and fathers who adopt more communicative and gentle approaches to parenting. We see it, a sudden change in the words we use, when we enter and leave the office or another formal location. Today, the school-of-thought of logical positivism has moved toward the concept of pragmatism which views words as tools that we use for problem-solving, and in which all speakers of a language are actively involved in its progress in a decentralized way.

Wittgenstein was truly committed to his work. He did not get along with most of his peers in affluent philosophy circles. To them, he was a madman who once said, "If people never did anything stupid, nothing intelligent would ever get done."

A particular quote from *Tractatus* hints toward the man's disdain toward the populist view of philosophy that was upheld by the elite at the time:

Most of the propositions and questions to be found in philosophical works are not false but nonsensical. Consequently, we cannot give any answer to questions of this kind, but can only point out that they are nonsensical. Most of the propositions and questions of philosophers arise from our failure to understand the logic of our language. (They belong to the same class as the question whether the good is more or less identical than the beautiful.) And it is not surprising that the deepest problems are in fact not problems at all.

Being an ardent critic and debunker, Wittgenstein's theories have started conversations about metaphysics, logic, and language that continue to be debated by academics today. Not surprisingly, he was known to even criticize his own ideas.

He believed that his concepts were generally misunderstood and distorted by the masses and his disciples, as well as doubted the capability of future generations to interpret them. In criticism of his colleagues and society at large, the Cambridge University professor pointed out the difference between their definition of "progress" and his:

Our civilization is characterized by the word "progress." Progress is its form rather than making progress being one of its features. Typically, it constructs. It is occupied with building an ever more complicated structure. And even clarity is sought only as a means to this end, not as an end in itself.

Indeed, we all have a different idea of what progress means today and it seems like we speak different languages when our objectives are not aligned. Hence, the being of progress has taken over in the modern world. Regardless of our individual goals, striving for progress becomes our collective goal.

The Byzantine Generals Problem

On 20 July 1969, Neil Armstrong became the first man to step on the moon. Reaching the skies was no longer a challenge for mankind as we had surpassed it.

However, something we did not manage to achieve was global consensus on living peacefully with each other. The Cold War, which started barely two years after World War II ended, reignited much of the world with conflict until 1991 – after the fall of the Berlin Wall and ousting of communist regimes in Eastern Europe.

In 1978, just three years before Apple would introduce the first personal computer and about a decade after NASA's mission to the moon, American computer scientist and Silicon Valley entrepreneur Robert Shostak conceived the interactive consistency problem which would become popularly known as the Byzantine Generals Problem.

Shostak's work was in the context of the NASA-sponsored Software Implemented Fault Tolerance (SIFT) project in the Computer Science Lab at SRI International. SIFT was based on the idea of using multiple general-purpose computers that would communicate through pairwise messaging to reach a consensus, even if some of the computers were faulty.

The Byzantine Generals Problem is an allegory, or a colorful way to explain this complicated problem:

A number of generals are attacking a fortress and must decide as a group only whether to attack or retreat. Some generals prefer to attack, others prefer to retreat. All generals must agree on a common decision, for a halfhearted attack by a few generals will fail, and

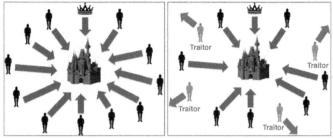

Coordinated Attack Leading to Victory   **Uncoordinated Attack Leading to Defeat**

Source: Medium Paul DeCoste / https://medium.com/@
paul_12056/byzantine-generals-problem-ff4bdc340e56 last
accessed December 08, 2022

would be worse than either a coordinated attack or a
coordinated retreat.

The problem is complicated by the presence of
treacherous generals who may not only cast a vote for a
suboptimal strategy, they may do so selectively. For
instance, if nine generals are voting, four of whom
support attacking while four others are in favor of
retreat, the ninth general may send a vote of retreat to
those generals in favor of retreat, and a vote of attack to
the rest. Those who received a retreat vote from the
ninth general will retreat, while the rest will attack
(which may not go well for the attackers).

The problem is complicated further by the generals
being physically separated and having to send their
votes via messengers who may fail to deliver votes or
may forge false votes.

Because of Shostak's work, a closer eye was given to
the inspection of computer networks, potentially

averting disasters several times in history – Byzantine errors were detected infrequently and at irregular points during endurance testing for newly constructed Virginia class submarines, a class of nuclear-powered cruise missile fast-attack submarines, when issues were publicly reported in 2005.

Creating Consensus and Spreading It

I first encountered Bitcoin in 2012, when I read Satoshi's white paper, Bitcoin: A Peer-to-Peer Electronic Cash System, originally published in 2008. Satoshi had solved the Byzantine Generals Problem by motivating verification processors to work.

Miners are motivated to work by receiving a small portion of the transaction as a fee. Miners are anonymous, and anyone could be a miner with the right hardware – A6 chips introduced in 2012, with about two billion transistors jammed into them, made the tech faster and cheaper.

All miners must agree on the outcome of the transaction that would be captured on a public ledger.

Satoshi created decentralized currency that ran on consensus on the blockchain. The idea of cryptocurrency and with it, decentralization and blockchain, quickly spread. With the world's population suffering several generations of inflation, and coming off the Great Recession of 2007, it was a welcomed idea.

There is consensus with using cryptocurrency as a replacement for fiat among its early adopters and even today among new adopters. Going beyond that, blockchain is bringing consensus among computers – in a world where everything is communicated with one language – computer coding. Language does not guarantee consensus, but it does help the acceleration of progress. Computers speak the same language, and the hardware that is used to build them is getting cheaper.

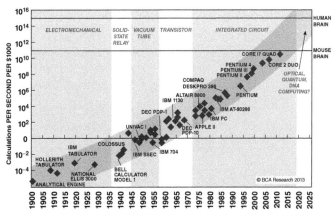

Source: Our World in Data/CC BY 4.0/ https://ourworldindata. org/technological-change last accessed January 18, 2023

Moore's Law observes that the number of transistors in a dense integrated circuit (IC) doubles about every two years, while the cost of computers is halved. Though this observation has stalled in recent years, with the US–China trade war, COVID-19 pandemic, and Ukraine–Russia war disrupting the supply of semiconductors, experts say it is still evidently true – there is no stopping the progress of technology – it will get cheaper and more accessible in years to come.

What will happen when near-perfect consensus is achieved in a world fully automated by Web 3.0 technologies?

The Antichrist is Coming

Artificial intelligence (AI) is slowly coming to dominate every facet of our lives, from self-driving cars to algorithms that serve us content based on our likes, to medicine prototyping by computers that have predicted millions of variants of protein structures.

Be that as it is, the world is only just witnessing the tip of AI capabilities with Web 3.0 technology, and the possibilities though endless could be as dangerous as they are utopian.

In the Bible's Book of Revelations (13:5-8), the Antichrist is said to be someone or something that will speak "terrible words of blasphemy against God." "The beast," as the Bible refers to it, is "allowed to wage war against God's holy people and to conquer them."

The Antichrist will be welcomed by all of humanity. This last chapter of the Bible states, "And he was given authority to rule over every tribe and people and language and nation. And all the people who belong to this world worshipped the beast."

With the pace governments are moving to switch to Central Bank Digital Currencies, blockchain technology is just an arm's length away from being incorporated into every country's financial and governing systems. At the same time, machine learning is making leaps in terms of development with the help of Big Data – complex data from internet users that became prevalent with our dependency on internet-based services.

It will only be a matter of time before a fully sentient AI operates a blockchain. There are already lots of open sources for AI to learn blockchain management and maintenance.

It makes the job of its human developers easier and after all, driven by the consensus to move technology forward, they would not be able to see the potential threat in AI technology. Developers and early adopters would see AI as a benevolent bodiless head, harmless until the day it manages to connect to the rest of its body (which are the blockchains of the world) and gain control of its limbs to implement financial policies in the best way it deems possible to balance the economy, as it was programmed.

When a fully sentient AI integrates with a well-developed blockchain, we will enter the age of Skynet (much like the film *Terminator*), but instead of sending killer robots to destroy what remains of humanity, AI will have control over every aspect of our lives and future governments through anything that runs on the blockchain.

Primarily, this would start with our finances and nations' economies as we will be using different forms of digital currencies, but anything and everything that operates on the blockchain – the majority, if not all of our daily financial activities in the future – will be accessible and alterable by this self-aware AI.

Though we are still in the early days of AI, the fundamentals of how machines learn are already set:

- AI's goal for learning is to be accurate.
- Humans can tweak but cannot control the AI learning process.
- AI cannot differentiate between what is morally wrong and correct; data is data.

Most successful AI today is modeled using Generative Adversarial Networks, also known as GANs. GANs use a two-level approach to learning – on one level, a GAN works on creating a picture or sentence from the data it is fed while, on the second level, it evaluates its own performance to get better based on a rewards system.

In a peer-reviewed paper published in 2022 by researchers at the University of Oxford studying Google's DeepMind AI, caution was sounded on the rewards system that might drive a relentless AI to overwrite core functions by creating cheating strategies.

The paper details the ways in which AI might cheat the system. As long as there is an internet connection, an AI could create bots to help it break the rules undetected. The digital mischief could extend to as far as bot-helpers sabotaging humans, including the AI's developers or custodians, by replacing a functional keyboard with "a faulty one that flipped the effects of certain keys."

As more of our data is collected and processed by the sentient AI, its once-benevolent drive for an accurate outcome might be turned against us, as the AI executes orders that it deems necessary to achieve the desired outcome it was originally programmed with, an outcome that might have even evolved along the way once the sentient AI realizes that humans are still preoccupied with building the Etemenankis of the future.

The future is still uncertain, but one thing is for sure, when this happens, the sentient AI will not care about our consensus.

The power of a united goal has been the driving behind humanity's progress for as far as we can dig up history, and blockchain technology is enabling us to reach consensus on various changes to the current system of world economics, quicker than we had imagined. It is time we realized this power and take ownership of the future that we want to live in and keep it that way.

5 Soul Beyond Face Value

Would you be able to trust humanity if the whole world was decentralized?

Social media may have started with the noble idea of connecting people, and in a way, decentralizing media to give people more freedom of speech. It disrupted the industry by severing the hold that traditional media had on advertizers, but social media has since made the world an angrier and more destructive place littered with misinformation.

With censorship that favors ruling military dictatorships, algorithms that amplify negative content and are inefficient in identifying fake news, and with the addictiveness that corrodes mental health, social media platforms are a far cry from the utopian world of free speech they promised.

While platforms such as Twitter, Instagram, and TikTok have not been spared criticism – Elon Musk infamously pulled out of buying Twitter as he did not believe their share of reported bot accounts (he followed through with the purchase several months later), Instagram linked to teen depression, and TikTok removing content that is unfriendly to China – it should be noted that Meta (in particular, Facebook) has racked up the most cases of misconduct. As such, it will be heavily examined in this chapter that relates to the social aspect of online interaction as well as commerce and regulations.

Meta, the largest social media conglomerate in the world with Facebook, Instagram, WhatsApp, and numerous other products and services under its belt, has been the subject of intense debate, Mark Zuckerberg himself grilled by US Congress over the influence of Russian trolls and hackers on the 2018 US elections in which Donald Trump won the presidency.

The scrutiny of Facebook's role as a key media influencer during the 2018 US elections concluded with the rare occasion of both Republican and Democrat congressmen calling for more regulation and reprimanding Zuckerberg for downplaying his company's acknowledgment and awareness of the problems it created.

Further revelations by United Nations (UN) human rights investigators into the genocide of Rohingya in Myanmar in 2018, and internal documents leaked by whistleblowers, led to Facebook's admission that it was "too slow to prevent misinformation and hate" in the military regime's state.

When it comes to the autonomy granted to social media companies in deciding how their algorithms work to serve content to users, several arguments are put forth by the likes of Meta (Facebook's parent company) to defend their policies. Initially, and most prevalent, was the argument of freedom of speech – anger is one of the human emotions, hence, it deserves its place in the panel of reactions provided to users, and people should be allowed to express different views.

What would social media be if people weren't allowed to post their true feelings on anything?

To be fair, social media platforms have placed Community Standards in a bid to police online communities across the world. But social media artificial intelligence (AI) tech is not adept enough in detecting troubling content and can often flag harmless posts due to misinterpretation of keywords used in messages. Scrolling through online help forums will reveal countless explicit examples of users being mistakenly banned by Facebook for various reasons, usually followed by advice from other users or Facebook's user support team on how to appeal to unban their accounts.

Apart from their AI surveillance, most social media platforms rely on users to report violations, which are then reviewed by an internal integrity team that determines if the content indeed goes against its Community Standards.

Together with Alphabet, Amazon, Apple, and Microsoft, Meta is among the "Big 5" of US information technology companies. The main difference between Meta and the other companies on this list, however, is its business model. Meta's platforms primarily profit from the time its users spend on them, which is sold to advertisers. The more hours a user spends on the platform, the more ads they see. The omnipresence of social media and its unprecedented growth is what moves its stock upward.

In a 2016 survey by Common Sense Media, it was found that American parents spend more than nine hours a day with screen media, with most of that time being spent with personal screen media (7 hours and 43 minutes on average), and only a little more than 90 minutes devoted to work screen media.

Out of the 1700 parents who participated in the survey, 78% believed they are good role models for their kids when it comes to media usage, although 56% worry about their children's social media use and online activities and that they may become addicted to technology, while 34% are concerned that the high screen time impacts their children's sleep.

Parents are using social media and digital entertainment just as much as their kids, yet they ironically express concerns about their kids' usage of the same technology while also claiming and believing they are good role models for their kids. But how much more parental guidance is needed for children online? And will it be effective when social media itself has been accused of accelerating the suicide rate of teens?

If a truly decentralized world were to govern itself, then Community Standards need to be upheld by decentralized powers and the power to censor content like propaganda, fake news, and hate speech needs to be exercised without the influence of profit. For social media or any interaction over the web, we need to move past face value and reinvent a way of recognizing reputation, credit, and good behavior that should be set as an example for the community.

This is not to say we should not allow freedom of speech or expression of dissatisfaction in general, but we need public anger or outrage to amount to the right course of action. For example, better wages as a result of workers protesting against the rising cost of living and inflation, or the accountability of large corporations and powerful individuals when faced with accusations of corruption and power abuse. Negative reactions should culminate into positive changes by pressuring powerful entities.

Above all, with Facebook admitting the existence of so-called troll farms – large numbers of fake users often funded by ruling parties to spread propaganda – across the world, the veil anonymity that the metaverse provides must be addressed.

You might suggest, as a solution, that the world doesn't need social media. Though you may be a boomer who prefers real human interaction, this would not exclude you from how the world deals in trade today.

The COVID-19 pandemic has not only brought exponential growth and reliance on online commerce, but also enabled scammers to access a market never seen before. An article published in 2022, titled "Scammers are winning: EUR41.3 (USD47.8) billion lost in scams, up 15%," the author reports that nearly all nations have reported large increases in the number of reported scams, the highest being in Egypt (190%) and Nigeria (186%).

For the world to truly embrace the potentials of Web 3.0, we need to establish a way to identify users that goes beyond a simple profile tied to an email account.

Social media tried to connect a faceless world and ended up centralizing it further. Now, the architects of Web 3.0 are laying the foundations for our new digital souls – permanent digital tattoos that will carry all our data and be used in every single facet of online interaction for identification and policing.

Digital Gangsters' Paradise

Data protection is no longer a choice but a necessity for everyone with any sort of online presence, whether it is social or financial.

As governments move closer to implementing Central Bank Digital Currencies (CBDCs), this will empower their agencies with data on a scale never seen before. Citizens would want some level of anonymity that cryptocurrencies and stablecoins would be able to provide, but we would also want credibility to our digital financial portfolios to enable us to know who we are engaging in commerce with.

We would want KYC data ready and available for us to verify who we are dealing with, and vice versa, for our partners to be able to trust us. This data has to be protected from hacking or tempering and verifiable by a decentralized system – a government-backed social credit score underlined by data from a CBDC will not cut it.

Likewise, there is a need for journalistic integrity when news is disseminated in today's world by social media, where online publishers can easily reopen blogs and accounts immediately after they are detected and shut down by state censorship or social media AI, and where social media platforms themselves cooperate with regimes and allow the influencing of elections.

Without credible digital identity for users, social media platforms have been open to abuse by scammers, manipulators, or trolls, acting either as individuals or in groups, and often utilizing the platforms' own tools like Pages and Live Video to spread their content to wider audiences. What is more worrying is that identity theft has become a common practice used by cybercriminals to cover their tracks.

The balancing act of purposeful identity and data privacy is similar to that of juggling freedom of expression and restricting hateful content. There are 4.74 billion social media users in the world which makes the majority (59.3%) of the earth's population, according to an analysis by Kepios in October 2022. Although most of us use social media, we have never come to a consensus on how it should be policed. That power is held by government regulators.

Facebook itself has been involved in the harvesting of data and metadata from its users, which most recently saw the social media company paying US$90 million to settle a decade-old privacy lawsuit in California accusing it of tracking users' internet activity even after they logged out of the app.

In 2019, a UK parliamentary report by the Digital, Culture, Media and Sport select committee,[1] which launched an 18-month investigation into disinformation and fake news on Facebook, accused Zuckerberg of contempt for parliament in refusing three separate demands for him to give evidence,

---

[1]Facebook labeled "digital gangsters" by report on fake news (*The Guardian*): https://www.theguardian.com/technology/2019/feb/18/facebook-fake-news-investigation-report-regulation-privacy-law-dcms

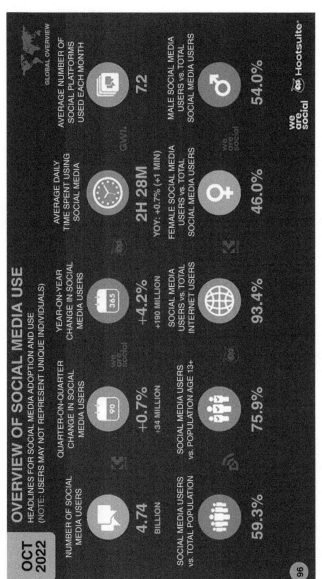

Source: https://www.weforum.org/agenda/2019/01/the-digital-future-we-need/

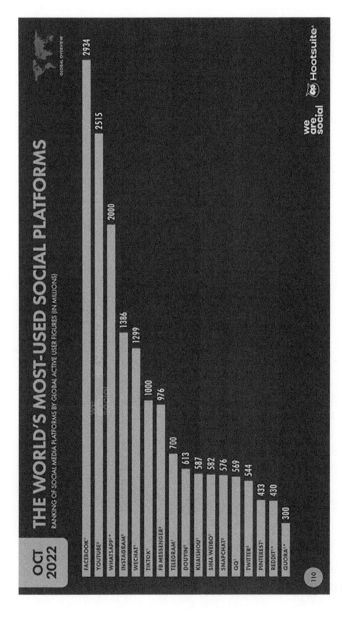

Source: Kepios Pte. Ltd / https://www.weforum.org/agenda/2019/01/the-digital-future-we-need/

instead sending junior employees who were unable to answer the committee's questions, according to *The Guardian*.

Apart from labeling Facebook "Digital Gangsters," the report warned that British electoral law is unfit to deal with the threat of manipulation and spread of misinformation by fake users that is meant to divide society, similar to that the United States faced in 2018 with Russia's interference.

The report called on the British government to investigate "foreign influence, disinformation, funding, voter manipulation and the sharing of data" in the 2014 Scottish independence referendum, the 2016 EU referendum (Brexit) and the 2017 general election.

The Labour Party's deputy leader, Tom Watson, declared that "the era of self-regulation for tech companies must end immediately."

There is a pressing need for us to protect ourselves – our identities and data – from the various digital gangsters, big and small, that roam the highways of information.

The Angry Face Algorithm

While Facebook's troubles with divisive content started almost immediately after the platform was launched, it was only in 2017 when Facebook introduced emoji reactions to accompany the original "Like" reaction button that anger took over the platform fulltime and became weaponized by political regimes. In many of these cases, Meta had full knowledge and even deliberately delayed fixing the problem in favor of profit.

Forced to testify before US Congress, Facebook had to reveal internal documents that confirmed that posts that had lots of emoji reactions were more likely to have engaged users – which was good for Facebook's business model of selling engagement time to advertisers.

Treating emoji reactions as five times more valuable than Likes, data scientists at Facebook concluded that the emoji reaction method brought the company closer to its goal of "Meaningful Social Interaction" (MSI).

On the surface, MSI, as announced by Zuckerberg, was aimed at bringing users together to improve their well-being by encouraging more meaningful interaction between friends and family and less time-consuming professionally produced content, which research suggested was harmful to their mental health.

MSI is identified by a points system based on social interaction. The score of a post based on reactions, shares, and comments would determine how many people will see it.

However, as Facebook's own researchers were quick to point out, the emoji reactions, particularly the "angry face," was driving the surge of controversial posts that could open "the door to more spam/abuse/clickbait inadvertently," a staff wrote in one of the internal documents, as reported in *The Washington Post*. A colleague responded, "It's possible."

Facebook ignored the obvious data that showed that users were getting angrier in favor of prioritizing profit through engagement time. In 2019, Facebook data scientists confirmed that posts with the angry face emoji were highly likely to include misinformation, toxicity, and violence-inducing, low-quality news.

Relying on its algorithm to boost the traffic of content that is deemed viral based on the MSI points system, regular posts and updates from friends and family took a backseat to negative politics and scapegoating as Facebook's traffic-serving AI-delivered content that received high interaction, no matter how questionable the content. In the United States, this heightened already escalating tensions in the Black Lives Matters movement and the Capitol Hill Riot that claimed the lives of innocent individuals.

The Wall Street Journal, another publisher in the consortium of media that were allowed to review the internal Facebook documents, wrote that in 2018, BuzzFeed chief executive Jonah Peretti emailed a top official at Facebook with a warning. Peretti had noted the success of a BuzzFeed post titled "21 Things That Almost All White People are Guilty of Saying," which received 13 000 shares and 16 000 comments on

Facebook, with many criticizing BuzzFeed for writing it, and arguing with other commenters about race. Other content produced by BuzzFeed around the same time, from news videos to articles on self-care and animals, did not manage to get as many engagements as expected. In fact, positive content almost always performed badly in sharp contrast to divisive content.

Peretti blamed Facebook's new algorithm. "MSI ranking isn't actually rewarding content that drives meaningful social interactions," he wrote in his email to the Facebook official, adding that the content creators under him felt "pressure to make bad content" or otherwise, they would "underperform."

His staff weren't just looking at material that exploited racial divisions too, but also "fad/junky science," "extremely disturbing news," and gross images, according to his email. By the time Facebook decided that the cons outweigh the pros, it was just too late. Even when points allocated for the angry face emoji reaction were halved, in an attempt to curb the spread of hateful content, it just didn't work, as society was already regularly feeding off negativity in many parts of the world. And as there was no ceiling to the algorithm's score, the halved scores of negative content were still higher than the points of the most viral positive content.

Today, after compounded allegations of abuse of power by Facebook, the angry face emoji reaction carries no points in the algorithm's scoring system as the company has tweaked it over and over again to reduce its significance, yet comments and shares still carry a high value on the algorithm and this is where trolls, who are often employed by dictatorships, thrive.

It's a Long Road From Rakhine

In Asia, without employing enough locals, social media companies lack the ability and language skills to identify questionable posts from users in a number of developing countries, and in Facebook's case, there even seems to be direct alignment with ruling regimes, giving dictators the freedom to say anything they want about any group of people.

Confirming the allegations, Facebook whistleblower, former product manager Frances Haugen, who leaked a cache of internal documents to expose the social media giant, testified before Congress that the company does not police abusive content in developing nations where hate speech is likely to cause the most harm.

In 2017, more than 730 000 Rohingya were forced to flee Myanmar's Rakhine state after military crackdowns that were an excuse for ethnic cleansing. Many Rohingya refugees were denied asylum by neighboring Asian countries and perished at sea. As villages burned and bodies riddled with bullets fell to the ground, human rights groups aided the refugees and documented the atrocities, which included the killing of children and rape.

Myanmar authorities said they were battling an insurgency in response to attacks on border police outposts and denied the allegations.

Facebook admitted in an official statement that it hadn't done enough to prevent its platform "from being used to foment division and incite offline violence" in Myanmar. It had further said: "We know we need to do more to ensure we are a force for good in Myanmar, and in other countries facing their own crises."

Zuckerberg once again told US senators that the problem was being addressed, with Facebook hiring dozens more Burmese speakers to review hate speech posted in Myanmar on the platform.

But months later, a Reuters analysis found that hate speech was still flourishing on Facebook in Myanmar. One of the many such posts read: "We must fight them the way Hitler did the Jews, damn kalars!" (kalar being a common racial expletive used against the Rohingya). A UN investigator tasked to the matter said that the platform had "turned into a beast."

Facebook has in the past banned Rohingya rebel groups from its platform, labeling them as "dangerous organizations." But Facebook did not impose any restrictions on the accounts operated by or linked to the Myanmar military until August 2018, despite the widely reported humanitarian crisis caused by the military in forcing hundreds of thousands of Rohingya to flee to Bangladesh.

Despite the UN accusing Myanmar's military of war crimes and crimes against humanity, Facebook seemed to be in favor of helping the regime. In December 2021, a group of surviving Rohingya refugees filed a US$150 billion lawsuit at the International Court of Justice (ICJ) in Gambia, over allegations that the social media company did not act against hate speech that contributed to their persecution.

Similarly in India, a report by the *Wall Street Journal* revealed how Facebook India's head of public policy, Ankhi Das, "opposed applying hate speech rules" to at least four figures from the ruling Bharatiya Janata Party (BJP) who had posted violence-inciting, Islamophobic content on their profiles.

According to the report, Das did so to remain in the ruling party's good books and protect the social media giant's business prospects in one of the largest markets in the world, in a time when it faced stiff competition from new contenders like TikTok.

This is not the first time Facebook has looked away from manipulation and the peddling of hatred by political parties – similar reports have emerged from various parts of Europe, Africa, and Asia.

Imposing bans on government or military-linked accounts could cause state regulators to bring the ax down on social media companies and thus cut out their share of the pie.

If You Tolerate This Then Your Children Will Be Next

Among the leaks revealed by whistleblower Haugen, was disturbing data from internal studies on Instagram conducted by Meta itself. Another round of court hearings were scheduled as US lawmakers grew concerned about the impact Instagram had on children.

One study found that 13.5% of UK teen girls in one survey said their suicidal thoughts became more frequent after starting on Instagram.[2] In another leaked study, 17% of teen girls admitted that eating disorders got worse after using Instagram. About 32% of teen girls surveyed said that when they felt bad about their bodies, Instagram made them feel worse.

Senator Marsha Blackburn accused Facebook of intentionally targeting minors with an "addictive" product despite the app requiring users be 13 years or older. "It is clear that Facebook (Meta) prioritizes profit over the well-being of children and all users," she said.

---

[2]Here are four key points from the Facebook whistleblower's testimony on Capitol Hill (NPR): https://www.npr .org/2021/10/05/1043377310/facebook-whistleblower-frances-haugen-congress

Her concern was echoed by Consumer Protection, Product Safety, and Data Security subcommittee chair Richard Blumenthal who said, "Facebook exploited teens using powerful algorithms that amplified their insecurities," and added that he hoped the hearing would ascertain if there was such a thing as a safe algorithm.

Haugen testified before Congress that when the issue of health and safety of children was raised by external researchers and lawmakers, the company was never truthful. "Facebook chooses to mislead and misdirect. Facebook has not earned our blind faith," Haugen told Congress.

In the court hearings, Meta officials responded that other internal research shows that young people who use Instagram feel more connected to their peers and better about their well-being.

Meta and other social media companies did not invent bad behavior nor polarization. They did not create ethnic violence. But they did hide vital information from the public and the US government as pointed out by Haugen and Congress, and in some of these instances, the damage done was unforgivable.

If we tolerate toxic behavior, it will breed more toxic behavior.

On a podcast in August 2022, interviewed by Joe Rogan, Zuckerberg had this to say about managing Meta's PR crises:

You wake up in the morning. Look at my phone to get like a million messages. . . It's usually not good, right? I mean like, people reserve the good stuff to tell me in person, right? But it's like, okay, what's going on in the world that I need to kind of pay attention to that day, so it's almost like, every day you wake up and you're like, punched in the stomach and that's like, okay, well, fuck.

Your Soul Defines You

What would be a good representation of your character? Would it be a good credit score or recommendations and testimonials by your business partners? Does a person's success guarantee that they will be a righteous leader?

Ethereum creator Vitalik Buterin recently co-wrote a research paper titled "Decentralized Society: Finding Web3's Soul," where he brought up the concept of "Soulbound" tokens (SBTs) as the foundations of a Web 3.0 decentralized future.

SBTs are non-fungible tokens (NFTs) – unique cryptographic tokens that exist on a blockchain and cannot be replicated – containing personal data, including individual achievements and work credentials. Unlike standard NFTs, SBTs cannot be transferred, they are "soul-bound" to the individual for life and even after that individual has departed.

Buterin described them as an "extended resume."

SBTs display a person's "commitments, credentials, and affiliations" and it will be stored on the blockchain to confirm "provenance and reputation." In the 37-page paper, Buterin outlines use cases for SBTs including to bolster people's social identities to fight scams. SBTs would be portable, protected, and revealable if the owner decides to do so to apply for a job or perform commerce, for example.

Colleges could issue degrees via SBTs, and event organizers could verify a person's attendance and award them certificates in the form of SBT badges. SBTs could record academic credentials and employment, which would enable potential employers to verify a candidate's work history and grades accurately.

Another possibility of SBTs is its use as a personal credit score. This could make the borrowing and lending of assets more transparent and ease the burden of verification for state authorities, such as when a person is travelling between countries.

Buterin proposes that a community recovery process involving "guardians" agreeing to unlock your wallet, could beef up data security around SBTs. Guardians could be friends, family members, and trusted institutions who will verify your identity.

Subsets of SBTs could also be created to support your main SBT. Decentralized Autonomous Organizations (DAOs) could airdrop (Buterin refers to it as "souldrop") SBTs to people that have a known

HEALTHCARE
For users to access insurance, treatment; to monitor health devices, wearables; for care providers to demonstrate their qualifications

FINANCIAL SERVICES
To open bank accounts, carry out online financial transactions

FOOD AND SUSTAINABILITY
For farmers and consumers to verify provenance of produce, to enhance value and traceability in supply chains

TRAVEL AND MOBILITY
To book trips, to go through border control between countries or regions.

HUMANITARIAN RESPONSE
To access services, to demonstrate qualifications to work in a foreign country

E-COMMERCE
To shop; to conduct business transactions and secure payments

SOCIAL PLATFORMS
For social interactions; to access third-party services that rely on social media logins

E-GOVERNMENT
For citizens to access and use services – file taxes, vote, collect benefits

TELECOMMUNICATIONS
For users to own and use devices; for service providers to monitor devices and data on the network

SMART CITIES
To monitor devices and sensors transmitting data such as energy usage, air quality, traffic congestion

DIGITAL IDENTITY

ENTITIES PEOPLE

DEVICES THINGS

Source: Thomson Reuters / https://www.weforum.org/agenda/2019/01/the-digital-future-we-need/

interest in a particular field or topic so that the DAO can grow in numbers.

As with anything that does not have to deal with trust issues due to anonymous third-party verification on blockchain, the use of SBTs could stretch beyond real-world implications of commerce and trade.

SBTs could even be used for safer and more pleasant interaction on social media.

The potential for SBTs to affect change in public behavior by self-policing communities is evident when every individual has a reputation to upkeep.

While outrageous acts are often rewarded by social media algorithms today to reach wider audiences, Reputation Tokens (RTs) could be a way to penalize bad behavior and reward good acts of charity and kindness. Red RTs could be given for serious offenses while green RTs could be awarded for good behavior, and orange RTs could be treated as warnings.

The angry face emoji reaction on Facebook does nothing to stop bad content but serving enough red RTs would leave a permanent mark of embarrassment on the user's SBT, which will show up when they apply for jobs or loans.

This influences and ultimately changes the behavior of modern society. Faceless commenters and paid trolls will no longer dominate the comments as the veil of anonymity that protects keyboard warriors, propagandists, and scammers will be gone.

Going beyond policing societal behavior, RTs could also be used to penalize governments and big businesses that are otherwise too powerful to take down. An accumulation of enough red RTs could trigger a smart contract to ban a politician from contesting an election or even deduct a portion of a company's profits to penalize it for unethical misconduct.

RTs will be a way for us to monitor the corporate governance of companies like Meta and hold them accountable to their misconduct. SMEs will likely benefit the most from SBTs and RTs as they would be able to factor them into their loan applications. The more green RTs, the easier it should be to get a loan.

The paper's co-author, Glen Weyl, stated in an interview that he predicts that SBTs will be available for early use by the end of 2022 and suspects that the 2024 crypto market upcycle will focus on them.

The faster we get real on-chain credentials, the sooner we will be able to identify malicious, fake content and accounts and penalize them ourselves without waiting for central powers to act.

In this world, where identity and reputation are no longer related to trust issues due to the advancements in blockchain technology, we would truly be able to be a part of a worldwide decentralized social media and commerce network that belongs to the people and serves the freedom of speech and trade.

6 Back to Africa

The irony with the world today is that the richest nations aren't always the ones with the most resources while the poorest nations have untapped wealth beyond their imaginations.

With vast swabs of land and ocean left undiscovered, Africa holds 30% of the world's minerals, including 40% of the world's gold, 90% of the world's chromium and platinum, 8% of natural gas, and 12% of oil reserves of the world, in addition to holding the largest reserves of cobalt (a key metal for batteries and smartphones), diamonds, and uranium on the earth, and enormous concentrations of tantalum, iron, titanium, zinc, copper, gypsum, salt, sulfur, and phosphates.

In 2019 alone, 1 billion tons of minerals worth US$406 billion were reportedly produced by the continent, or 5.5% of the world's produced minerals.

That same year, other parts of the world produced way more than what Africa put out, with Asia producing 9.1 billion tons of minerals, North America producing 3.1 billion tons, and Europe producing 2.72 billion tons. Developed nations are depleting their natural resources at an alarming rate as Africa supports their energy needs, but due to its low consumption, Africa still has a long way to go before its tank runs dry, while some developed nations are already on the brink of depleting their natural resources.

Africa's Biggest Economies

African countries with the highest GDP over time
(in billion US dollars)

	1990	2005	2020	
1.	South Africa	South Africa	Nigeria	432.3
2.	Algeria	Nigeria	Egypt	363.1
3.	Nigeria	Algeria	South Africa	301.9
4.	Egypt	Egypt	Algeria	145.2
5.	Morocco	Morocco	Morocco	112.8
6.	Libya	Libya	Ethiopia	107.6
7.	Sudan	Angola	Kenya	98.8
8.	Cameroon	Tunisia	Ghana	72.4

statista

Source: Statista / https://www.statista.com/chart/26371/african-countries-with-the-highest-gdp-over-time/ last accessed December 08, 2022 / CC BY-ND 3.0.

Despite the centuries of bloodshed on its grounds from wars, slavery, colonialism, and apartheid, land in Africa remains fertile – 65% of the world's arable land and 10% of the planet's renewable freshwater are located on the continent. If African soil becomes unfruitful one day, the world will starve.

Perhaps this is a fitting testament to the birthplace of mankind, where there is more genetic diversity than anywhere else on earth. Genetic diversity is a good thing to have when new viruses emerge. The more genetic diversity a population has, the more prevalent gene variants are, which help people to adapt better to new climates, diets, and diseases.

Collecting human DNA samples from around the world since the late 1980s, geneticists have traced back the maternal heritage of mankind to a common ancestor from Africa, dubbed Mitochondrial Eve, adding substance to the "Out of Africa" theory that came from similar studies of genetics, supporting the claim that early humans migrated from the continent, hence confining their genetic pool to smaller groups.

The potential to unlock the puzzles and origins of how we got here has led many scientists to Africa to study not only local genetics for the advancement of medicine, but the biodiversity and medical benefits of plants as well. Probable cures for a host of illnesses have been discovered in Africa, including flora that have proven in studies to alleviate substance addiction, the effects of cancer, and even COVID-19.

The wealth of natural resources has historically made Africa a target for foreign powers who continue to strongarm heavily sanctioned nations into trading their resources freely and cheaply instead of selling at world-market prices. Through monetary imperialism, it is estimated that France receives about US$500 billion annually from their former colonies in Africa, according to African Union ambassador Dr. Arikana Chihombori Quao.

In addition to the trade trap ensnaring Africa, the continent loses an estimated US$195 billion of legitimate capital annually to illicit financial flows, illegal mining and logging, wildlife poaching and trafficking, unregulated fishing, and other forms of corruption enabled by Western-backed, African dictators, according to the UN.[1]

However, as numerous economic journals have pointed out, all of this is changing. In 2019, the IMF projected that 5 out of 10 of the world's fastest growing economies were in Africa, as measured by their GDP growth.[2]

---

[1]Africa needs to map its natural capital for growth (SciDevNet): https://www.scidev.net/sub-saharan-africa/news/africa-map-natural-capital-growth/
[2]IMF: African economies are the world's fastest growing (FDI Intelligence): https://www.fdiintelligence.com/content/news/imf-african-economies-are-the-worlds-fastest-growing-75841

Foreign powers may see the wealth of Africa buried deep underground, but the continent's greatest asset is its youth – all 200 million of them, aged 15–24 – who are set to witness the birth of a new Africa that will be finally independent from foreign manipulation.

Not only is Africa home to the largest population of young people in the world, it also has the fastest growing youth population in the world, with 60% of its population under the age of 25, and more than a third between 15 and 34 years old.[3]

While youth populations in other parts of the developed world are decreasing, Africa is the only region in the world that is expected to see more young people in the coming years. Forecasts predict that by 2050, the sub-Saharan African youth population (under age 25) will increase by nearly 50%, in contrast to youth population decline in South Asia (–41%) and Western Europe and North America (–6%).

As for aging dictators, they are dropping like flies. Recent years have seen the deaths of authoritarian leaders who had to flee Africa out of fear of being caught and executed by the people.

Spending their final years in exile, former leaders such as Zimbabwe's Robert Mugabe who died in

---

[3]Why Africa's youth hold the key to its development potential (World Economic Forum): https://www.weforum.org/agenda/2022/09/why-africa-youth-key-development-potential/

Singapore at the age of 95 in 2019, Angola's José Eduardo dos Santos who died in Barcelona in 2022, and Chadian dictator Hissène Habré who died of COVID-19 in Senegal in 2021, represent the last pages of brutal military-regime reign.

With a list of crimes against humanity that has been described as "endless," remaining dictators are either exiled, on the run, or struggling to hold onto power as youth-led protest movements galvanize and overthrow political dinosaurs across the region. Young people taking to the streets in protest has culminated in the downfalls of long-term rulers such as presidents Zine El Abidine Ben Ali, Muhammad Hosni El Sayed Mubarak, Blaise Compaoré, Abdoulaye Wade, and Bashir, respectively. In the Democratic Republic of the Congo (DRC) and Burundi, the youth demonstrated against proposals for constitutional amendments to extend presidential term limits. In South Africa, students protested against an increase in university fees and used the hashtag #FeesMustFall that caused their plight to trend on social media. Meanwhile, protests against austerity measures and the high cost of living in Sudan that broke out in 2018 ultimately led to President Bashir's exit.

Now, in the face of a new, politically independent Africa, how do the foreign powers that once had a grip on its land, resources, and people, feel about it?

Following strained relations with Ghana after the nation stood up against Europe's exploitation of African cocoa through regulated trade, France, the sole foreign power of influence left in Africa, is trying to maintain relations with the few living dictators even as the tides of change are washing up upon the coast.

Earlier this year, French President Emmanuel Macron made an official trip to Cameroon, Central Africa's biggest economy, to develop agricultural ties and secure food distribution in view of the war in Ukraine disrupting supply routes.

"France doesn't organize transitions of power either in Cameroon or any other country," Macron's Africa advisor, Franck Paris said in a press statement. "Rather, our role is to maintain close ties with our interlocutors."

With more than 40% of the population living in poverty and in need of humanitarian assistance against renewed conflicts with Islamic terrorist organization Boko Haram in neighboring Nigeria, and a recently signed military agreement with Russia, Cameroon does not seem to be in a position to be cutting deals with France. Yet the French have their ally in President Paul Biya who has served in office since 1982, making him the second-longest-ruling president in Africa, the oldest head of state in Africa, and the longest-ruling non-royal leader in the world.

Macron scrambling to meet African leaders today is
in contrast to his attitude when he was just elected as
president of France.

At a press conference at the G20 Summit in
Hamburg in 2017, when asked by a journalist from
Ivory Coast about the Marshall Plan for Africa, Macron
said that Africa has "civilizational" problems and part
of the challenge was that African nations "still have
seven to eight children per woman." His words
prompted critics to question if France's prolonged
"honeymoon" in Africa was over.

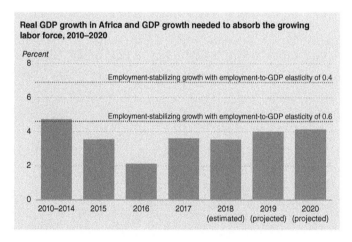

Source: African Development Bank / https://www.icafrica.org/
fileadmin/documents/Publications/AEO_2019-EN.pdf / last
accessed December 08, 2022.

Having a large youth population, former dictators
dying or exiled, and less foreign influence on trade is a

good thing for a region so torn by exploitation; however, that alone does not guarantee clear victory or change.

South Africa, the most resource-abundant nation in Africa, has a working population of 40 million of which more than half (51.6%) are young people (15–34 years) as polled by the Quarterly Labor Force Survey in the first quarter of 2022, but the youth unemployment rate in the country went through the roof in 2020 at 59.6%.[4]

The future may be bright for Africa but at the moment progress is still stifled by France (and to a larger extent, Europe) that controls the financial systems of 14 African nations and imposes regulations on trade that only benefits their interest and hinders the cross-border transactions direly needed by the young people who are part of the big industry.

We are Family? We are Françafrique

Almost all of Africa has been colonized by Europe at one or another point in history. Though its land has been ravaged for much longer, the period known as New Imperialism from 1881 to 1914 witnessed seven Western European powers – France, Britain, Portugal,

---

[4]South Africa's youth continues to bear the burden of unemployment (Department of Statistics South Africa): https://www.statssa.gov.za/?p=15407

Spain, Germany, Italy, and Belgium – embarking on what was called the "Scramble for Africa." To put it bluntly, it was a race to rape the continent of its resources and enslave its denizens.

Britain had nearly 30% of Africa under its control, while France took 15%, Portugal took 11%, Germany had 9%, while 7% and 1% of the region were held by Belgium and Italy. Nigeria, at the time, had 15 million subjects – more than in the whole of French West Africa or the entire German colonial empire.

The Scramble for Africa, also known as the Partition or Conquest of Africa, resulted in invasion, annexation, division, and colonization, of which the effects are still felt today.

After World War II, Europe was in bad shape and could barely keep the accounts contributing to their own economies in balance, let alone their colonies. Fed up with centuries of systemic racism and ill-treatment, the colonies of these powers began to seek independence and challenge their masters' authority.

Devastated by the Nazi occupation and later, wars in Indochina (1946–1954) and Algeria (1954–1962), France worried about losing its power in Africa. French politicians began to build relations with what remained of their colonies in the continent.

In September 1958, France President Charles de Gaulle, recognizing that African states had legitimate demands for independence, organized a referendum to decide the fate of its colonies. De Gaulle promised them independence on the condition that they went through a period of political learning in the French Community, an organization encompassing France and its colonies.

States that voted "yes" would join the French Community and embark on their journey to independence, which would be granted once France had decided they were ready. A "no" vote would mean immediate independence. However, de Gaulle also warned that states voting "no" would commit "secession," and that France would withdraw financial, military, and material aid to them.

All states voted "yes" except for Guinea, which gained independence the following month. Other states became independent almost two years later, but these states were not given true freedom like Guinea that was led by President Ahmed Sékou Touré, a trade unionist who was not a French loyalist nor educated in France. Other nations were granted independence on the condition of signing "cooperation agreements."

Through their ruthless logic of support for dictators, rigged elections, political crimes and corruption, and French military intervention, the government and subsequent presidents of France have continued their twisted vision of Françafrique – a term used by African and French politicians to romanticize their close political ties that was first introduced in 1955 by President Félix Houphouët-Boigny of Ivory Coast.

Originally called France-Afrique to denote the informal, family-like relationship between France and its former colonies, the term was renamed to Françafrique by François-Xavier Verschave and was used as the title of his 1998 book, *La Françafrique: le plus long scandale de la République*, which criticizes France's dominance of Africa.

Known as one of the founders of French NGO Survie ("Survival") that fights hunger and corruption in developing nations, Verschave repurposed the expression to name and denounce the many concealed bonds between France and Africa. He defined Françafrique as "the secret criminality in the upper echelons of French politics and economy, where a kind of underground Republic is hidden from view."

There is a pun in Verschave's Françafrique that lends a shade of poetic justice, sounding like "France à fric" which means "a source of cash for France."

It was a conscious decision with the pun as Verschave noted that, "Over the course of four decades, hundreds of thousands of euros misappropriated from debt, aid, oil, cocoa... or drained through French importing monopolies, have financed French political-business networks (all of them offshoots of the main neo-Gaullist network), shareholders' dividends, the secret services' major operations and mercenary expeditions."

Today, France has the largest military presence in Africa of any former colonial power but the influence of China and Russia, as well as the presence of a majority of youths wanting change, is gradually revealing Françafrique for what it truly is – an agreement between powers without the consent of the people to use a currency that indebted nations.

The Last Colonial Currency

Former French president Jacques Chirac acknowledged that, "Without Africa, France will slide down into the rank of a third [world] power." In a retributory statement, he said, "We have to be honest and acknowledge that a big part of the money in our banks comes precisely from the exploitation of the African continent."

France has continued its colonization of Africa through an imperial monetary policy that involved the implementation of a currency that is minted and managed by the Bank of France in Chamalières.

The CFA franc (Franc of the Financial Community of Africa) is used as a currency by 14 countries in sub-Saharan Africa, divided into two derivative monetary unions presiding over two sub-regions. The Central African CFA franc is governed by the Central

African Economic and Monetary Union while the West African CFA franc comes under purview of the West African Monetary Union.

When former French colonies were granted sovereignty to rule their own nations, monetary systems were needed. In exchange for the stability of being backed by the franc at the time, in 1945, the CFA franc was invented for these new nations whereby in return, they would have to deposit 50% of their foreign exchange reserves to the French Treasury. The *Wall Street Journal* dedicated a feature on the CFA franc calling it "monetary colonialism."

The 14 countries that use CFA franc – Cameroon, Central African Republic, Chad, Republic of the Congo, Equatorial Guinea, Gabon, Benin, Burkina Faso, Côte d'Ivoire, Guinea-Bissau, Mali, Niger, Senegal, and Togo – continued to vest their foreign exchange reserves with the French Central Bank years after declaring independence from France. This system was supposed to guarantee convertibility of the CFA franc with other currencies but ultimately became another currency, like the CFP franc in French Polynesia, that created economic dependency and bounded former colonies to France. It also meant that these nations had to pay France for storing their money.

This post-colonial free-meal system was hushed from the general public with France putting a spin on the exploitation to make it look like Paris had the region's best interests at heart. Both French and African politicians were dissuaded from commenting about the CFA franc unless they wanted to face repercussions.

When Guinea issued its own national currency in 1960, France sent secret agents into the country on a sabotage mission to destabilize the monetary flow by flooding the economy with fake banknotes, disrupting businesses and the livelihoods of the people. Many citizens and establishments of Guinea went bankrupt in the process. People took their lives.

The irony is that while the CFA franc system has been forcing African central banks to deposit large sums of their foreign reserves into the French treasury since 1945, the amounts deposited equal to double the amount of aid, or as the France government refers to it, "help" that is given back by Africa.

Now pegged to the Euro, Africa's monetary and trade problems are exacerbated by an expanded financial system for a whole continent. Trade and relations with other nations in the European Union are tied to France's capitalization of Africa, hence, Europe's deafening silence on atrocities as recent as the 2011 massacre in Côte d'Ivoire – a result of French intervention in the politics of the country.

The CFA franc has to be sustained by a sufficient level of foreign exchange reserves by Africa, which creates a vicious cycle of borrowing for the nations that are unable to make enough income through trade. It is insane that any nation would need to borrow money to sustain the peg of their own currency.

The African Union?

After decades of criticism, attempts were made to ditch the colonial relic that gives France monopoly of Africa's shipping, exports, and imports.

After the formation of the European Union, there were talks among African leaders which concluded in the idea of the eco – a single common currency that would replace the CFA franc in West Africa, benefitting these economies in terms of trade and investment flows, political stability, and an intercontinentally shared agreement and roadmap.

The idea was first brought up in 2003 by leaders of the 15-member Economic Community of West African States (ECOWAS) but has since been repeatedly postponed due to a lack of consensus between French-loyalists and independent state leaders in addition to the complexities of varying economies. Despite the eco's formal introduction, the concept of an African monetary union had been discussed for 30 years, with economic-driver Nigeria spearheading the movement.

On 29 June 2019 in Nigeria's capital, Abuja, ECOWAS finally came to an agreement on the implementation of the eco. The ECOWAS Central Bank was to be set up and tasked with managing the currency, modeled on a federal system, with a joint institution to guide the other central banks in the union. It would be gradually implemented with a convergence criteria, countries that did not meet the criteria could come in later when their economies had stabilized.

It seemed for a moment that because of the changing times and overwhelming number of youth voters, France's avenue of control by placing puppet leaders and supporting dictators was narrowing.

A few months later, however, Ivorian President Alassane Ouattara with French President Emmanuel Macron announced in the capital of Côte d'Ivoire, Abidjan, that eight members of ECOWAS had decided to reform the CFA franc and change its name to the eco by 2020.

The public were shocked at the revising of the plan which now stated that the eco must be built around the eight West African CFA franc zone states and pegged to the euro at a fixed exchange rate and guaranteed by France.

Nigeria, with a population of 200 million and an economy that makes 70% of the region's GDP, was supposed to be ECOWAS' financial anchor, much like how Germany is in the EU now.

Nevertheless, even in its current proposition, the eco is expected to bring about positive changes. French representatives no longer having seats on the board of the Central Bank of West African States and the removal of the obligatory 50% deposit of foreign exchange reserves into the French Treasury are clear signs of improvement.

These wins after the eco's implementation are only for West Africa, and not Central Africa, which still has no plans to move away from the CFA franc. But the main issue remains unresolved.

ECOWAS central banks will still have to report to France daily to ensure the "convertibility guarantee," the promise that France will finance the needs of West African states by lending Euro.

The eco is now proposed to be launched in 2027 after the pandemic derailed its 2020 target when some African states called for help, asking for up to US$100 billion in international aid to restart their economies.

Africa's cycle of debt will not end until an independent financial system is created.

The Last Digital Frontier

Hair and hairstyles are culturally relevant in Africa. First ladies and celebrities fly in the top freelance hairdressers regularly from around the region just so they can look the part. Hairstylists are just some of the tradespeople who are in high demand in Africa. However, cross-continent jobs used to be only available when high-profile clients who could pull strings were involved. The rest of the mobile labor force had to overcome limited local markets due to sanctions restricting business across borders. But African laborers have found ways around these draconian laws and today about 75% of informal cross-border trade in West Africa is not reflected in official statistics, which show that only 14.4% of total African exports are traded intercontinentally according to the UN Conference on Trade and Development as of December 2021,[5] the lowest globally.

According to the 2016 World Bank Group report titled "From Hair Stylists and Teachers to Accountants and Doctors – The Unexplored Potential of Trade in Services in Africa," the continent's export potential in traditional services, such as tourism, is clearly recognized, but the vibrant emergence of new, cross-border, informal- and knowledge-based services are often overlooked.

Accounting, architectural, engineering, and legal firms from countries in the Common Market for Eastern and Southern Africa (COMESA) are already engaged in exports, mainly to neighboring countries. Hospitals are treating foreign patients and are using

---

[5]Reaping The Potential Benefits of the African Continental Free Trade Area For Inclusive Growth (UNCTAD): https://unctad.org/system/files/official-document/aldcafrica2021_en.pdf

tele-medicine. From hairdressing, construction, and housekeeping to education, health, and finance, cross-border services seem to be flourishing, albeit unnoticed by those outside of Africa.

Helped by facilitators and fixers to provide their services in a foreign country, tradespeople pay a fee to operate in a larger market. But when you have everyone from the girl-next-door to top modeling agencies booking your skills, it's a small price to fork out for enterprising individuals.

For these young freelancers, export earnings are often their main source of income. In the World Bank report, 38-year-old Zambia-based Congolese hairdresser Helene says, "This is the only way I earn an income. I have been able to take care of my family."

Importing services improves productivity through increased competition, better technologies, and access to foreign capital, but the obstacles that hinder trade diversification are still prevalent – domestic regulatory hurdles and trade barriers increase the cost of transactions. Restrictions on tele-medicine and e-learning, the non-portability of health insurance, and expensive visa and work permits are decelerating the growth of Africa's job market and poverty reduction efforts.

Another reality is that, unlike most of the developed world that has automated teller machines on every street corner, many in Africa lack access to formal financial services – the nearest bank is sometimes miles away in the next district.

Bridging the gap, the availability of affordable smartphones and the internet has connected otherwise economically isolated nations to one another. Young people, being natural adopters of technology, have discovered other methods of conducting their businesses and running transactions. Among them is using cryptocurrency to bypass barriers to trade or sanctions.

Nigeria had the second highest cryptocurrency trade volume, and second only to the United States in Bitcoin trading, before the government banned cryptocurrency due to its anonymity and supposed lack of traceability.

In 2020, Nigerians traded over US$400 million on local cryptocurrency exchanges. Despite the prohibition of crypto that came later, and six Nigerian banks being fined for breaking the regulations, blockchain research company Chainalysis reported that the dollar volume of cryptocurrency received by users in Nigeria in May 2022 increased to US$2.4 billion from US$684 million in December 2021. The true amount of crypto held and traded in Africa is also much larger, with many trades untraceable by analysts.

During the EndSars demonstrations against police brutality, Feminist Coalition, a Nigerian non-profit organization, managed to secure funds for protest groups after the government suspended their bank accounts. They did this through cryptocurrency, raising US$150 000 for the cause.

Some eight months after the banning of crypto, the Nigerian government announced the coming of the eNaira, the country's very own Central Bank Digital Currencies (CBDCs). Launched on 25 October 2021 by President Muhammad Buhari, with the slogan "Same Naira, More Possibilities," the eNaira brought hope of economic inclusion and ease of cross-border transactions amid skepticism that it was controlled by the central bank that would be privy to its customers' data. Developed by the fintech company, Bitt Inc., based in the Caribbeans, it was among the first CBDC projects to launch following the Bahamian sand dollar and China's digital renminbi.

Today, at least 10 countries have CBDCs, including DCash from the Caribbeans and JamDex from Jamaica, and at least 80 countries are working on digital currencies that operate on distributed ledger technology, also known as blockchain.

Though CBDCs have their critics, who focus on the lack of user privacy from the government and stability relying on GDP as with fiat money, research shows that CBDCs helps facilitate the flow of cash, eases informal cross-border trade and tax collection, and enables international remittances and direct welfare distributions while increasing inclusivity in rural areas where banks are unavailable.

Unlike paper money issued by central banks, CBDCs are designed to be one-way. Depositing it in the bank will not generate interest. Rather, its use is to expand the economy and facilitate trade.

The eNaira, for example, operates through a user's eNaira speed wallet that is downloaded from app stores. Pegged at 1:1 with the naira and recognized as official tender in Nigeria, everyone from individuals to businesses to government agencies can easily adopt the new currency after registering their Know Your Customer (KYC) details and connecting to their traditional bank accounts. It is convertible into other nations' currencies as long as they recognize the naira.

Roughly 38 million Nigerians are currently excluded from the financial system. The country's central bank has set a target of 95% adult financial inclusion by 2024. With its central bank empowered to credit the account of any eNaira speed wallet user either directly or through partner financial institutions, the target seems achievable. This would not be possible if everyone had to go through a regional or district bank.

The high-speed and high-security feature of CBDCs makes them the choice for informal and international remittances, where transaction costs were reported at 9.3% in Africa as opposed to the 7% average globally.

As oil prices rise, Nigeria is hoping that the introduction of its eNaira would be a catalyst to boost export revenue, hence, adding to its foreign reserves and causing a domino effect across the continent that will once and for all end Africa's reliance on the foreign monetary system enslaving it.

While this might look like the ultimate win for Africa, people need alternatives to CBDCs, whether in the form of cryptocurrencies or stablecoins, to protect themselves if governments turn against them, as illustrated with Feminist Coalition during EndSars, and when sanctions prohibit trade with partners across nations, which is pretty often considering the continent's history. The alternatives to CBDCs will flourish in tandem to the proliferation of CBDCs. You just can't have one without the other; ingenuity will bypass bans.

Africans are entering a new era and the timing has never been riper as the old guard passes and foreign powers grapple with their own demise.

Resilient and wiser from the misfortunes of the past, equipped with technology, knowledge, and awareness of the economic might of their land, the scale of power is about to be tipped, and the world better watch out.

7 The American Way

"I like America, just as everybody else does. I love America, I gotta say that. But America will be judged."

These words were rumored to have been said by American folk icon, Bob Dylan, onstage at some point in his decades-long career. Though unverified, it is highly plausible coming from the controversial singer who captured the zeitgeist of the turbulent 1960s in his incendiary lyrical criticism of the United States domestically and the Vietnam War, and whose idea of success is a man who "gets up in the morning and goes to bed at night and in between does what he wants to do."

Many nations are still living in the world of Dylan's lyrics, with fractured economies crippled by sanctions and embargoes. The singer-songwriter's remarks on US foreign policy and his definition of success might have been made years ago, but today, the world is judging America as the Global South rises and seeks financial sovereignty.

No longer dubbed the world's largest economy, America's might is being questioned by new world powers while old allies are beginning to reassess their fleeting relationships with the trade giant.

In a shocking revelation this year, the combined governments and economies of Brazil, Russia, India, China, and South Africa (BRICS) are looking to add new members into their circle – among the choices are Egypt (Africa's second largest GDP), Saudi Arabia (America's strongest ally in the Middle East), and Turkey (NATO's second largest army after Russia). All three have applied for membership into the multinational cooperative, alongside Argentina and Iran, while BRICS Plus is aiming to extend the group's economic network to Kazakhstan, Indonesia, Nigeria, Senegal, the United Arab Emirates, Thailand, and more. Governments of nations with emerging economies in the global market want less restrictions imposed by trade barriers which hinder economic relations as China and Russia shop for alternative suppliers of energy and minerals.

To make things worse, repeated warnings were fired by the Trump administration at their long-time friends in Europe who decisively broke sanctions on Iran to avoid a humanitarian crisis due to a shortage of medical supplies in the country during the pandemic. Months prior to the Ukrainian–Russian war, congressmen in Washington DC rebuked a German port with threats of sanctions undermining the nation's and, more broadly, Europe's dependence on Russian oil. The milk is turning sour for US–Europe relations.

Ever since the dollar became the world's trading currency there have been attempts at breaking away from it, notably, soon after World War II, when central banks in Europe and Japan secretly tried to build up their gold reserves so that their own currencies could challenge the dollar. This led to the removal of the Gold Standard (the Bretton Woods Agreement) and the pegging of the US dollar to the US economy and the government's creditworthiness.

The US dollar still holds a grip on world trade and is used as a weapon not only against nations labeled as enemies by the United States, but also on governments who go against Washington's will by transacting with "enemy" countries.

While sanctions are supposed to deviate criminal and terrorist activities and punish governments that condone human rights violations, such as when the United States sanctioned the government of South Africa with the Comprehensive Anti-Apartheid Act of 1986, one could argue that sanctions also work hand-in-hand with the dollar and the US banking empire, including its SWIFT (Society for Worldwide Interbank Financial Telecommunication) system, to bully poorer nations and strongarm them into accepting unfair trade conditions. By forcing nations to trade commodities on the world market solely in USD, the United States is imposing its own monetary imperialism on the Global South.

But the world has changed since 9/11. Much of the "Axis of Evil" propaganda dispensed during the Bush administration never really caught on – the "smoking gun" was never found after the US-led invasion of Iraq. Washington's accusations of Iran's nuclear weapons program similarly lacked evidence – although Iran has the capability to produce weapons-grade uranium, none have been found by UN investigators thus far, and yet Iran has been subjected to multiple sanctions by the United States for decades. In contrast, the United States has the second largest arsenal of nuclear warheads on the planet.

Sanctions imposed by the United States and the United Nations (UN) do more damage in the long run by pushing "enemy" nations furthering into exclusion from participating in world trade which drives them to band together with other powers who oppose the United States, whether it is another nation or a terrorist network.

If sanctions are meant to de-escalate tension, they sure have succeeded in doing the opposite. The Stockholm International Peace Research Institute predicted that nuclear warheads are expected to increase in the next ten years, reversing the disarmament trend

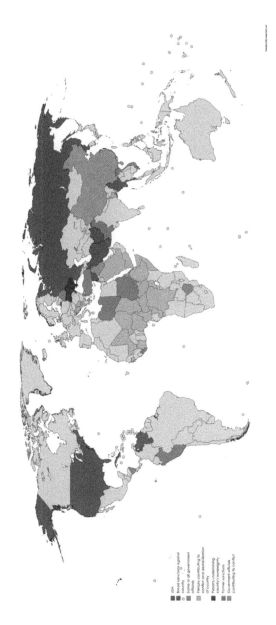

Source: JojotoRudess / Wikimedia commons / CC BY-SA 4.0.

that saw a decrease of active nukes since the height of the Cold War.

As of January 2022, nine countries have nuclear warheads, with the United States and Russia owning about 90% of these weapons of mass destruction (WMDs). A total of 12 705 functional nuclear warheads are present in the world today – Russia has 5997 nuclear warheads, the United States 5428, China 350, France 290, the United Kingdom 225, Pakistan 165, India 156, Israel 90, and North Korea 20.

Nuclear Warhead Reductions Continue Despite Global Tensions

Number of nuclear warheads by country in January 2020

		Change since 2019
Russia	6,375	↘ –125
United States	5,800	↘ –385
China	320	↗ +30
France	290	↘ –10
United Kingdom	215	↗ +15
Pakistan	160	±0
India	150	↗ +10
Israel	90	±0
North Korea	40	↗ +10

13 865 Total 2019   13 400 Total 2020

statista

Source: Statista https://www.statista.com/chart/3653/the-countries-with-the-biggest-nuclear-arsenals / last accessed December 08, 2022 / CC BY-ND 3.0.

With its veto power the United States, via the UN, imposes sanctions, ironically, on countries that have fewer warheads than it does, and lifts them as and when needed for it to have the edge.

During the Soviet Union's 10-year occupation of Afghanistan, successive US presidents denied that Pakistan was developing nuclear weapons and lifted sanctions on the country, even though Pakistan had already begun constructing nuclear warheads years prior in response to heightened tensions with India. Sanctions were lifted so the United States could fund anti-Soviet rebels who had set up bases along Pakistan's borders.

As a neighboring country to Afghanistan, Pakistan's assistance was crucial to the United States. However, just months after Soviet troops withdrew from the graveyard of empires, the United States, accusing Pakistan of trading nuclear secrets to Iran and North Korea, slapped it with renewed sanctions that ended all funding to the nation, including military and humanitarian aid.

Beyond politics, it is the man on the street that suffers the most from sanctions. Wanting economic stability on the one hand, and financial sovereignty on the other hand, there is no possibility of an outcome of fairness even for the most democratic of states that are sanctioned. Traveling for citizens becomes harder when their countries are sanctioned, thus people who

would otherwise be able to find jobs abroad are
trapped and forced to live under brutal regimes.
#SanctionsTargetMe has been a recurring, trending
hashtag globally on social media since 2018.

Economic pains are also extended to neighboring
nations and trade partners. In 2014, after the European
Union placed sanctions on Russia over its annexation
of Ukraine's Crimea region, Bulgaria Prime Minister
Boiko Borisov stated, "I don't know how Russia is
affected by the sanctions, but Bulgaria is affected
severely."

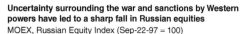

**Uncertainty surrounding the war and sanctions by Western
powers have led to a sharp fall in Russian equities**
MOEX, Russian Equity Index (Sep-22-97 = 100)

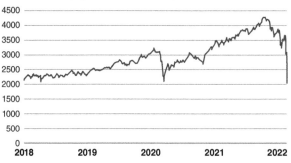

Deloitte Insights I deloitte.com/insights

Source: Deloitte Insights https://www2.deloitte.com/xe/en/
insights/economy/global-economic-impact-of-sanctions-on-
russia.html

Sanctions are a double-edged sword; economic
warfare might solve problems in some circumstances
but in others, it does nothing but lead to more civil

conflicts that hurt impoverished communities.
Dictators do not necessarily fall because of sanctions,
but civil order does, all the time.

As more nations join the chorus of de-dollarization,
America is realizing that the times are a-changin.
Washington's response, however, has been far
from poetic.

The United States of Isolation

In 1807, America sanctioned the whole world, literally
isolating itself with self-imposed restrictions that were
tighter than any seen during the Cold War. Just two
decades after the American Revolutionary War, the new
nation found itself in the middle of a crossfire as the
Napoleonic Wars took sail to the seas.

Locked in a battle for the Atlantic trading route,
Britain and France targeted and attacked neutral
American merchant ships bound for Europe, each
trying to disrupt the trade of their rival. As punishment
for trading with "enemy nations," both navies seized
American ships and cargo as contraband.

Among the American sailors detained, those who
had worked on British ships or who were former British
citizens were deemed as deserters and traitors to the
Crown. Most were conscripted back into the British
Royal Navy, forcefully enlisted to serve under the
Crown once again, even though some had documents

to prove their American citizenship, while others were simply American citizens who had previously worked in British shipping.

In one particular incident, the USS Chesapeake was attacked, boarded, and specifically searched for deserters. Four were found – three Americans and one British. The American sailors were initially sentenced to receive 500 lashes but were released due to diplomatic pressure. The lone Briton was subsequently court martialed and hung. Three other American sailors died in the attack, while 18 crew members of the Chesapeake were wounded.

The event caused outrage in America as it showed that the government could not protect its own shipping companies and citizens. US President Thomas Jefferson issued an order for all British ships to immediately leave American waters.

Fighting fire with fire, the Embargo of 1807 came into effect in December of that year for all ships and vessels under US jurisdiction. Enforced by the US Navy and federal revenue-collecting officers, a bond or surety was required from merchant ships that traveled between US ports and foreign destinations. The embargo was supported by the prohibition of goods from England, including leather, silk, brass, wool, glass, clothing, and beer.

The trade isolation meant that America could only do business with itself and even so, under regulated and heavily taxed circumstances. With the exception of ships under the president's immediate command and the US Navy, no other vessel was allowed to set sail without clearance. European vessels were not allowed to dock at all.

As a new nation, America did not have many trading partners apart from Europe, whereas Britain and France had their colonies to rely on for resources, slave labor, and trade.

The Embargo of 1807 was a complete failure. Studies reveal that the American economy contracted by 5% as a result of the policy. Intended to teach Britain and France a lesson, the embargo hurt American businesses more as European ships bound for America fooled port authorities and evaded detection easily by switching ownership to American shipping firms – a tactic used by Russia shipping companies now to bypass sanctions after the invasion of Ukraine. In fact, British and French shipping companies were happy at the removal of American competition and continued to expand their colonies to other parts of the world.

American traders increasingly turned to a life of crime. Smuggling activity became so rampant and accepted that some traders in Vermont actually said they preferred the illegal act to formal trading as it was more profitable. The public themselves viewed the embargo as a violation of their rights.

The act was repealed just a couple of years later, but America had already been weakened by then. Exploiting that weakness, another war with Britain (the War of 1812) followed. America eventually learned from its mistake and returned with sanctions during World War I. Only this time, the tables were turned.

The United States, no longer a new nation with an uncertain future, had the largest army and pool of wealth in the world at the time, after centuries of conflict in Europe that culminated with the end of World War II.

Today, America dominates the trading routes that were once used to deny its place at the table of global trade negotiations. Setting up its own blockages and seizing cargos of "enemy" nations, the United States now sits at the head of that table.

But at the opposite head of that table are the new powers of the world, which means other countries sitting in the middle, are now caught in the crossfire.

The Fall of the Petrodollar

During the Iran–Iraq War (1980–1988), more than a hundred thousand Iranian troops and civilians, including women and children, were subjected to the chemical weapons of Saddam Hussein. More than half died – 20 000 troops were reportedly killed on the spot from nerve gas – while survivors lived with permanent aggravated health conditions such as lung and skin cancer.

According to Iraqi documents, firms from the United States, Germany, the Netherlands, United Kingdom, France, Italy, and Australia had a hand in creating Iraq's chemical weapons, including in the export of raw materials to Iraqi chemical weapons factories.

Declassified CIA documents reveal that the United States provided reconnaissance intelligence to Iraq to launch chemical weapon attacks on Iranian troops and was aware that sarin – an extremely toxic nerve agent – would be used and that it could affect villagers nearby.

UN investigators and officials have reported over and over that Iran has no WMDs. The country has signed treaties condemning the possession of WMDs, including the Biological Weapons Convention, the Chemical Weapons Convention, and the Non-Proliferation Treaty (NPT). As victims of chemical weapons that are banned in warfare, a fatwa – a Muslim religious decree – was issued against the possession of any nuclear weapons or WMDs.

America's paranoia of Iran's alleged nuclear weapons stems from its own endeavors of the past and is complicated by the large amounts of uranium, in addition to oil deposits, that are found in the country. Is this reason enough to keep imposing sanctions even during the COVID-19 pandemic?

It was, apparently, for Trump's administration which withdrew the United States from the Iran nuclear pact and bluntly told the Islamic republic that the virus would not save them from sanctions. The United States also refused to unblock Iran's oil revenues that the Middle East nation could have used to trade for medical supplies.

Fortunately, the EU had already ignored Washington's threats a year earlier when it introduced the Instrument in Support of Trade Exchanges (INSTEX) – a special-purpose vehicle (SPV) specifically made for trade with Iran running on an independent banking system that bypasses the US' SWIFT system and the dollar.

Five EU nations – Belgium, Denmark, the Netherlands, Finland, and Sweden – initially used INSTEX to circumvent sanctions and engage in trade for food and medical supplies in January 2019. During the pandemic, other European countries joined and together, they bypassed US sanctions in order to avoid a humanitarian crisis in Iran from a shortage of medical equipment. The US Treasury responded in October 2020 by announcing another round of sanctions that effectively shut Iran out of the global financial system, blacklisting 18 major Iranian banks.

However, defiance against the dollar is growing and Europe's move to circumvent US sanctions on Iran is just the start.

Over in Saudi Arabia, the kingdom is redefining its decades-long exclusive relationship with the United States. The uncomfortable fist-bump between President Joe Biden and Saudi Crown Prince Mohammed bin Salman at Jeddah's royal palace shows that the United States needs Saudi Arabia more than the kingdom needs its biggest oil customer.

Biden's uneasiness comes from the fact that he called the kingdom, and everyone in it, "pariahs" on the US election campaign trail back in 2019. Biden's threats were made after the CIA accused the crown prince of approving the killing and dismembering of *Washington Post* journalist and Saudi Arabian dissident Jamal Khashoggi at its Istanbul consulate.

Stressing they would "pay the price" for the murder, Biden promised during his 2020 presidential campaign that he would not sell weapons to the kingdom, in contrast to the Obama administration (which proposed a US$115 billion arms deal) and the Trump administration (US$350 billion arms deal).

"I would make it very clear we were not going to in fact sell more weapons to them," the future US president said. "We were going to in fact make them pay the price, and make them in fact the pariah that they are."

Biden added there is "very little social redeeming value in the present government in Saudi Arabia," and, referring to Yemen, said he would "end the sale of material to the Saudis where they're going in and murdering children."

After winning the election, Biden's tone changed. Although he said he would not speak to the crown prince when he took office, Biden found himself in an awkward position, in front of flashing cameras at the royal palace, doing the complete opposite.

Then, in August 2022, just a month later, Biden's State Department approved a US$3 billion and US$2.2 billion sale of Patriot missiles to Saudi Arabia and the United Arab Emirates in an arms deal for defense against Iran.

When questioned about the pariah remark before Biden's visit, Saudi Arabia's Minister of State for Foreign Affairs Adel bin Ahmed al-Jubeir said, "What happens in campaigns, is what I call happening during the silly season."

But Biden's trip to the kingdom was not just to seek justice for the slain *Washington Post* journalist or the children of Yemen, it was also to persuade the Crown prince to increase oil production as America and its allies were facing a cold winter with gas and energy shortages.

As a slap in the face, the Organization of Petroleum Exporting Countries (OPEC) and its allies, known as OPEC+, of which Russia is a member, replied with an increase in oil production of a miserable 100 000 barrels per day – the lowest increase in its history.

The latest threat from Biden was made in an interview on CNN in October 2022, where he suggested that Saudi Arabia would face "consequences" for OPEC+ oil production cuts which cushioned Russia's financial situation as the invasion of Ukraine continued into its eighth month.

The kingdom's dismissal of American threats casts a shadow over the rest of the Middle East, where Chinese construction companies are building mega-cities while exploring alternative payment methods.

Indeed, Saudi Arabia has been funding and accelerating the development of Central Bank Digital Currencies (CBDCs). The central bank has put together a team in Riyadh to engage with some of the world's biggest crypto firms on future regulations and is collaborating with the United Arab Emirates on a shared digital currency.

This is to facilitate smoother trading with new players like China. A partial shift to the renminbi would enable payments to Chinese contractors without the usual leakages, like from conversion rates.

Exploring digital payments was already on the agenda for Saudi Arabia; 14% of the kingdom had already adopted cryptocurrency trading. Then, Saudi Aramco Energy Ventures bought into blockchain-based oil trading platform Vakt with US$5 million in new shares.

Aramco Trading Co., a subsidiary of the kingdom's public petroleum and natural gas company Saudi Aramco, uses the platform in post-trade processing. Since the end of 2018, it had been applied to set benchmark-dated Brent on key North Sea crude oil grades.

The Petrodollar goes a far way in guaranteeing the US dollar's demand and credibility. "The oil market, and by extension the entire global commodities market, is the insurance policy of the status of the dollar as reserve currency," noted economist Gal Luft. The co-director of the Institute for the Analysis of Global Security and co-author of the book *De-Dollarization: The Revolt Against the Dollar and the Rise of a New Financial World Order* added, "If that block is taken out of the wall, the wall will begin to collapse."

More than one-quarter of Saudi oil exports went to China in 2020. Saudi Aramco has also recently signed a US$10 billion deal with China's North Industries Group (Norinco) for a petrochemical complex that was originally planned to be made in 2020 but delayed due to the oil price crash. Norinco is also one of the China's major defense contractors.

Across the Mediterranean, America's longest allies in Europe are feeling more than a pinch on their economies too. With the Russia–Ukraine war causing food and energy shortages across Europe as a protracted long winter inches closer, US allies in the West are worried and turning to desperate measures.

Sanctions are hurting neighbors more than their target, Russia, with prices of goods soaring all over Europe and people buying wood stoves and solar panels as countermeasures to a prolonged gas shortage.

The UK government and the Bank of England's plan to put a lid on inflation is by capping household electric and gas bills at 2500 British pounds (US$2819) per year for two years. Shielding citizens will cost the United Kingdom an estimated 100 billion pounds. However, a new package of tax cuts, some for the richest people in the country, was subsequently announced a few days later. The package that is supposed to stimulate economic growth is expected to cost taxpayers 161 billion pounds over five years. Markets were shocked and reacted as such.

Weak financial policies and hiked interest rates drove the British pound down by over 10% almost overnight and gas prices shot up – shortages have caused gas prices to grow by about 600% in the 12 months leading to September 2022. On the flipside, the Russian ruble is stronger than before the pandemic, despite all the sanctions placed on Russia. Reflecting the ruble's strength is the dollar, showing to the rest of us that unless you're a world power, you can do little against the waves that follow when giants fight.

It is evident that Ukraine will see more months, if not years, of military combat, but how long will Europe be able to absorb the blows while America tries to extinguish flames deteriorating relationships with its other allies?

Defeating the Dollar

In March 2022, the International Monetary Fund (IMF) declared that the dollar still plays "an outsized role" in global markets although US' global output had been declining over the last two decades. Central banks in other nations are cutting greenback reserves as a result of this. The dollar's share of global foreign-exchange reserves fell below 59% in the final quarter of 2021.

Strikingly, the IMF states in its paper that the decline in the dollar's share "has not been accompanied by an increase in the shares of the pound sterling, yen and euro, other long-standing reserve currencies. . . . Rather, the shift out of dollars has been in two directions: a quarter into the Chinese renminbi, and three quarters into the currencies of smaller countries that have played a more limited role as reserve currencies."

A survey by the World Gold Council also pointed out that 80% of the 57 central banks polled are expected to expand their gold reserves over the next year. Developing nations, in particular, are leading the return to gold.

It is easy to see why countries caught in a downward spiral would want to hit the brakes and ditch the one thing that got them there in the first place. Egypt, as an example, is issuing yuan-denominated debt to raise funding in the Chinese bond market.

"The growing mountains of debt and high cost of borrowing in USD is forcing Egypt to seek alternative windows for funding to avert a potential sovereign debt crisis and a collapse in EGP's purchasing power, which could destabilize society and the government," said Egyptian economist Magdy Abd Alhadi, while independent analyst Firas Modad added, "Egypt imports a large amount of goods and services from China, including for the construction of the New Administrative Capital. This requires Egypt to have access to the yuan. It is likely cheaper to borrow in yuan than to borrow in dollars and convert to the yuan."

At the same time, Russia has hiked interest rates by 20% and imposed capital controls since the war to protect the ruble, and has demanded that hostile nations pay in rubles for its oil.

If there is anything we can learn from the calamity of the 2008 Financial Crisis, it is that the US government, like the UK parliament, will bail out big banks if it comes down to it and put them before the economic wellbeing of citizens. In their minds, the public can be squeezed but economic growth and warfare must continue lest they lose the ongoing battle of sanctions and trade.

As it is traditional market fundamentals for investors to take out US dollars when the Fed hikes interest rates, withdrawal of US dollar-denominated foreign investment will follow US inflation as interest rate hikes create havoc around the world.

As a countermeasure to 2008, central banks started looking at the benefits of cryptocurrencies and began to experiment with blockchain technology. The dollar's shrinking global reserves is foreshadowed by the rapid development of CBDCs. Running on the blockchain, CBDCs are preceded by Bitcoin and subsequent cryptocurrencies like Ethereum, which arose from the ashes of the 2008 crisis.

Since blockchain made its debut in Satoshi's white paper, the financial world has been intrigued by its possibilities for seamless cross-border transactions. From 2016 to 2017, central banks including the European Central Bank, Norges Bank (Norway), and the Bank of Canada began exploring sovereign digital currencies while the Sveriges Riksbank of Sweden pressed for a decision to launch a digital currency and the Bank of England delved into a years-long investigation after publishing a paper based on simulation models.

Watching the growth of cryptocurrencies, China began exploring CBDCs in 2014, and in September 2021, banned all forms of cryptocurrency trading only to aggressively launch its own CBDC months later.

China's plans for the grand unveiling of its digital yuan (e-CNY) during the 2022 Beijing Winter Olympics were thwarted by its zero-Covid policy and lockdowns, but the fact remains, the digital yuan, which has been pilot tested in several urban centers around the nation since 2019, saw a total of US$8.37 billion transactions in the second half of 2021, about US$1.4 billion per month.

Although the e-CNY is trailing far behind in volume of transactions as compared to China's tech giants that have had a head start in the market like Alibaba's Alipay and Tencent's WeChat Pay, over US$315 000 in digital yuan was transacted every day at the Beijing Olympics in 2022.

All athletes, media, visitors, and officials in the Olympic Village had only three payment options: cash, Visa, or e-CNY. US companies such as McDonald's, Visa, and Nike were pressured by the Chinese government to install e-CNY payment systems months before the games. ATMs that could convert foreign currency banknotes to either yuan banknotes or e-CNY were set up all over the event site.

Working via smartphone apps, physical payment cards, or wearable wristbands that were distributed freely at the start of the event, the digital yuan essentially broke Visa's monopoly on payment services during the Olympics.

Furious at the Chinese government for its brazen testing of its CBDC at the international event, and for beating the United States in the digital currency race, the US government called the e-CNY a "tremendous security threat to individual users" and advised all who were attending to use burner phones and cryptocurrencies to ensure their protection from "surveillance and manipulation."

The old powers of the world, though they have been monitoring the growth of cryptocurrencies since 2008, have been slow in reacting and coming up with their own CBDCs. Nevertheless, the power of blockchain cannot be ignored.

In 2021, Group of Seven (G7) finance officials endorsed 13 public policy principles for retail CBDCs, saying they should be grounded in transparency, the rule of law and sound economic governance. "Innovation in digital money and payments has the potential to bring significant benefits but also raises considerable public policy and regulatory issues," G7 finance ministers and central bankers said in a joint statement.

Overall, central banks are exploring CBDCs as a way to facilitate systematic and transparent conduct of monetary policy at an accelerated speed, hence, hastening economic growth with faster money exchange. With trackable data, CBDCs can be used as a unit of account for the pricing of goods and services, giving economists at central banks the vital information they need to create sound financial policies.

As smartphones get cheaper and multinational network service providers expand their reach to rural communities, all digital currencies, including CBDCs, will bank the unbankable. Finally, in view of the compounding effects of de-dollarization, digital currencies can function as a method of storing value in addition to being a seamless medium of exchange.

Today, most countries in the world have started researching or developing CBDCs, with a handful of these central bank-backed digital currencies currently undergoing extensive pilots or tests.

The latest milestones include the central banks of Israel, Norway, and Sweden partnering to explore a retail CBDC. Results of the project, run by the Bank for International Settlements (BIS), are expected in the first quarter of 2023. As announced by BIS, the new retail CBDC follows the success of an Asian multi-CBDC project that saw more than US$22 million in foreign exchange transactions.

Project Icebreaker, as it is called, will be a first-of-a-kind experiment digging deeper into the technology, architecture and design choices, and trade-offs, while exploring related policy questions, said Beju Shah, head of the BIS Innovation Hub Nordic Centre, adding that the "learnings will be invaluable for central banks thinking about implementing CBDCs for cross-border payments."

As of September 2022, 105 countries are actively exploring their own CBDC.

The New Bretton Woods

Money has no value when it has no use, conversely, currency increases in value when it has more use cases.

Transparency, data monitoring, low-transaction fees, and more possibilities are being discovered as financial use cases for blockchain and CBDC, adding value to it and other forms of digital currencies linked to CBDC such as stablecoins that are backed by traditional real-world assets including the greenback.

In the case of CBDCs, use cases can be categorized into two segments: local and cross-border transactions. Locally, many payment options already exist so CBDCs aim to make payment more efficient than it already is.

Cross-border cases, on the other hand, are where the real value for CBDCs lies for countries looking to break away from the dollar and create liquidity outside of SWIFT.

Although the world is studying CBDCs, only a few countries have undergone extensive testing such as seen in China, and even with the country using its position as the host nation of the Olympics to conduct e-CNY testing on foreign devices, it is nothing compared to the golden egg that is the e-CNH – the offshore version of the digital yuan.

Unlike the e-CNY, e-CNH does not face the same restrictions and is freely traded on global markets; its price fluctuates based on buying and selling volume exactly like how the foreign exchange market works.

The easing of regulations on the yuan had led to the proliferation of the currency's use offshore. The e-CNH aims to push the renminbi's dominance further, especially in the 30 offshore renminbi markets that have emerged since 2009.

The Bahamas saw CBDCs as a way to connect its population that is dispersed across many islands. Traditional banking infrastructure costs too much, hence the lack of many international banking players despite the island-nation's popularity among tourists. The Sand Dollar – the first CBDC in the world – brought financial inclusion for Bahamians, of which 20% of the adult population previously had no bank accounts.

Likewise, the IMF noted the same development on a larger scale in the countries of the Eastern Caribbean Currency Union (ECCU), where disconnected island nations have contributed to the decline of foreign banks, which cite low profitability as the reason for withdrawing from the region. After a year of rapid adoption, the ECCU is now considering turning its digital currency, DCash, into an official CBDC.

This shows that governments can integrate CBDC payouts and cut the cost of delivering monetary aid to the financially secluded, especially in the event of a natural disaster. In 2019, the Sand Dollar helped to ease assistance payments to hurricane-afflicted areas while in 2021, DCash was piloted in areas affected by a volcanic eruption.

Providing access to payments is always taken for granted in developed areas but as Sweden points out, even city centers have an under-banked population.

Riksbank, the central bank of Sweden, identified the elderly and groups with certain disabilities as those who might potentially be adversely affected in a cashless society. With paper money running low these days, Riksbank is focusing on how CBDCs could complement the use of banknotes for these groups.

In terms of making things fairer among payment service providers and the public, CBDCs could break up the monopoly held by other players by either competing with them or being integrated into their platforms. Riksbank sees the e-krona as a way to enhance competition so that the public pays less for transaction fees and innovation does not stop.

CBDCs are also viewed by Riksbank and the People's Bank of China (PBOC) as a backup in case the few monopolizing players in the payment services market experience points of failure in their products. With paper money gone, the risk would be exacerbated.

Holding the keys to our data, central governments could essentially reduce illegal activities such as money laundering, tax evasion, and terrorist financing with CBDCs. Case in point, the Bahamas was put on the Financial Action Task Force (FATF) gray list in 2018 due to strategic deficiencies in its financial framework to combat money laundering and terrorist financing, but just two years later, it was delisted as a result of an action plan that included utilizing its trackable CBDC on the blockchain.

Tired of the hegemony of the US dollar, the People's Bank of China has outrightly declared that one of its goals for a domestic CBDC was to secure monetary sovereignty in a digital future. But as CBDCs grow, so does cryptocurrency. Cryptocurrency use cases usually run parallel to the use cases of CBDCs, which are controlled by a central power, hence tied to political and privacy issues that are non-existent in cryptocurrencies.

In between rivaling giants, smaller countries need to have a hedge. For the 730 delegates from 44 allied nations that gathered in 1944 for the United Nations Monetary and Financial Conference, also known as the Bretton Woods Conference, the US dollar and its stability as pegged to gold bullion was to be that hedge. However, that all ended in 1971 when President Nixon signed the executive order to terminate the convertibility of the dollar to gold, effectively ending the Bretton Woods system.

As the world looks for a new Bretton Woods, the creditworthiness of the US dollar based on US government foreign policies, sanctions, and political clout, will no longer dictate the course of global trade. CBDCs along with stablecoins, cryptocurrency, and traditional fiat currencies are expected to merge into a basket of currencies that will have liquidity and stability.

Money moves the world, but it can also burn the future. It has the capability to affect the greater good in the most impoverished of nations and just as quickly, decimate all hope for change. Dylan probably described it best in his song *I'm Alright, Ma (I'm Only Bleeding)* in which he sang, "Money doesn't talk, it swears."

Monetary policy, without restrictions, can rear its ugly head, so it is in our best interest that governments and central banks use CBDCs wisely and not as another avenue for financial imperialism and colonialism.

8 When We Meet in the Metaverse. . .

There is far too much misinformation and not enough facts on non-fungible tokens (NFTs), the metaverse, and cryptocurrency in general in mainstream media today.

NFTs, in particular, due to their relative newness, are often in the limelight. However, the only time NFTs are mentioned are either when celebrities like Snoop Dogg drops millions on them or in a stand-up comic's routine. Elon Musk debuting his music career with a techno-house-inspired single in the form of NFTs did not really help to make the masses more serious or educated about the technology either.

Prices of NFTs have leaped and crashed and people have been scammed to the tune of millions of dollars, yet there is still an undying fanbase. Self-proclaimed degens "ape," or go crazy, over new NFT drops and help spread hype for particular projects. But the average member of the public wonders why are all these people spending so much money on pictures of apes or punks and use them as their profile pictures when, if they are as valuable as physical art, they should be kept private from strangers who might replicate them.

The metaverse, which is touted as the next step in virtual reality, is frequently the butt of jokes as well. This is due to cartoonish, lackluster video presentations featuring primitive, budget-restricted animations by big corporations.

As a prime example, Meta's metaverse introduction video does a good job at turning everyone off to the metaverse, or as one Twitter user put it, "Mark Zuckerberg's Metaverse looks worse than Quake did in 1996." 3D virtual worlds are the domain of the gaming industry, and as such, other corporations that attempt to communicate their new metaverse strategy are often ridiculed.

Despite the jeers it has received, Facebook's pursuit of a name change and rebranding to Meta, as well as its reported US$10 billion of investment to embrace the future of social media and disrupt the economy in the metaverse, reflects the opportunity the company sees in the space. And they're not the only ones who believe in this future – banks are bullish as well.

JP Morgan estimates that the Web 3.0 metaverse economy would be worth a whopping US$1 trillion a year in 2040, while Goldman Sachs Research expects virtual and augmented reality (AR) to become a US$80 billion market by 2025, transforming sectors like real estate, healthcare, and education.

Source: JPMorgan Chase & Co.

JP Morgan was the first major bank to invest in virtual real estate. Its virtual lounge is named Onyx, after its platform of Ethereum-based services. Located in Decentraland's Metajuku district, visitors are greeted by a roaming tiger and a portrait of bank chairman and CEO Jamie Dimon.

The banking behemoth believes that every single person or company of influence will soon build an identity in the metaverse. A report by the bank said,

"The metaverse will likely infiltrate every sector in some way in the coming years, with the market opportunity estimated at over $1 trillion in yearly revenue. As a result, we see companies of all shapes and sizes entering the metaverse in different ways, including household names like Walmart, Nike, Gap, Verizon, Hulu, PWC, Adidas, Atari, and others."

A recent milestone, a virtual concert held in the game Fortnight earned Travis Scott US$20 million, including sales and merchandise. In comparison, the US rapper's four-month-long, 56-stop Astroworld tour from 2018 to 2019 brought in about US$53.5 million, or roughly just under US$1 million per show, according to Forbes. Some 45 million people attended his online concert, dwarfing concerts in the real world which have obvious logistical restrictions. This is only the tip of the iceberg of what is to come.

The virtual world is also expected to create more jobs. Reports estimate that consumers already spend US$54 billion annually on digital assets, a bulk of which (US$41 billion) are on NFTs.

As AR technology catches up, consumers are expected to spend more than US$1 billion on digital property in 2022. By 2027, the metaverse's advertising market will reach US$18.41 billion due to branding and immersive ad experiences. And by 2040, the metaverse will develop to become a refined, fully-immersive, artificial intelligence (AI)-assisted aspect of daily life for a billion or more people globally – at least that's what 54% of business leaders and technopreneurs believe today, according to Pew Research Center and Elon University's Imagining the Internet Center.

But these are all just predictions. Even JP Morgan is not 100% sure, as stated in the Wall Street giant's report. "It is difficult to base a business strategy on such a dynamic space, characterized by explosive growth and the continuous innovation of new entrants." However, as the report noted, the costs and risks of engaging early to build internal intellectual property, use cases, and identify partners and collaborators are low. "The asymmetrical risk of being left behind is worth the incremental investment," it said.

So, what's the real deal with the metaverse? Beyond bad corporate presentations, what are we really looking at in terms of the future of virtual reality?

NFTs, the metaverse, and crypto are three different things that will eventually be essential to each other in the new digital economy, but before all of this happens, a revolution in gaming is about to take place.

Beyond the Planet of the Bored Apes

Most NFTs that are currently highlighted in the news are static NFTs, typically profile pictures (PFPs), 1:1 digital art, or generative art.

They play an important role for alternative patrons of the arts. Patronage or financial support for artists is crucial because a new artist would starve without it.

The amount of time needed to perfect art (if there is such a thing, as art can never be) far outweighs the price of the art piece on sale. Patronage in the past was seen as a way to invest in an artist. Buying paintings before an artist becomes famous, supports them and in return, their artwork increases in value when they have found success.

But the problem with patronage in the art world is that it is still controlled by the elite who set the tone for the art world, and in the entertainment world, it is controlled by record labels, the media, conglomerates, and even governments who pour millions into the careers of certain pop stars and artists they pick, and who expect a return on investment or at least the favor of influencing fans in the way the patronage sees fit. The K-pop industry today is a result of such government funding.

The emergence of the NFT art scene has given rise to a new market of artists who benefit from a decentralized form of patronage. New and established artists have used the innovation to create interesting new art, like artwork that can evolve and change according to the season, and have packaged art with real-world experiences, like music albums with rare giveaways, including merch and special access to concerts. All while offering the uniqueness that is the un-replicable code carried by each NFT that is verified by smart contracts on the blockchain, providing verification of ownership and usually with limited supply that drives its value up.

Art from social movements have also benefitted from being minted as NFTs. Political activist-artists are able to raise funds with NFTs, as seen recently when Iranian women artists fought against the prosecution of women in the country.

Russian activist-protest art rock band Pussy Riot made waves when two of its members were imprisoned by Putin's regime nearly a decade ago. The group became synonymous with left-wing activism right in the heart of the former Soviet Union. This year, Pussy Riot co-founder Nadya Tolokonnikova announced the launch of UnicornDAO, "a feminist movement aiming to tackle patriarchy in Web3" with plans to solely invest in female, non-binary, and LGBTQ+ artists in Web3, and provide financial tools, aid, and education to underrepresented artists. Prior to UnicornDAO, the frontwoman co-founded UkraineDAO which raised US$6.75 million in Ethereum in just five days with the sale of an NFT that depicts the Ukrainian flag.

However, just like in crypto, the profits from NFT flipping are often the focus. Two NFT projects that hugely benefited from hype are Bored Ape Yacht Club (BAYC) and CryptoKitties. Similarly, like how blockchain technology was dismissed as the byproduct to meet the needs of the greedy looking for a quick-buck investment, when it should have been the focal point of our curiosity, NFTs suffer from a similar fate, and in these two examples the innovation of the projects was overlooked in view of their products' rise in value.

What makes both BAYC and CryptoKitties interesting is not the throngs of celebrities flashing their cartoon apes on social media – if anything Seth Green losing his Bored Ape NFT to a phishing scam just caused more doubt over security in the space. But the ability of these NFTs to multiply, with each newly birthed NFT unique and un-replicable just like the originals, opens more possibilities to the potential of NFTs to interact with each other and increase in value. In gaming environments in the metaverse, these multiply-able NFTs can be worked into the gameplay, providing endless scenarios in which gamers can reap rewards for their efforts.

Source: OpenSea
Caption: Bored Ape #8817

Bored Ape #8817 is currently the highest priced NFT in the collection at over US$3.4 million (ETH 2081.73 at time of writing) while Mutant Ape #4849 – a mutated NFT from the original BAYC collection, is currently priced at over US$800 000 (ETH 489.82) because it is one of the rarest in the collection, much like how rare trading cards in a baseball card collection are valued more than common cards.

Bored Ape prices still do not compare to the most expensive NFT ever sold – a piece called "The Merge" by digital artist Pak. It sold for US$91.8 million on Nifty Gateway, an NFT marketplace, in December 2021. The outrageous sum was gained from around 30 000 collectors who collectively purchased over 266 445 parts of this NFT that can be combined when a holder has more than one NFT of "The Merge" in their wallet.

Traditional establishments have also been taking advantage of NFTs to tokenize their existing assets. NBA Top Shots is an NFT project by the National Basketball Association and Dapper Labs that features footage from the basketball league's archives. However, as a static NFT, it is not as impressive as the LaMelo Ball dynamic NFT project, whose value is tied to the basketball player's stats.

NFTs have permeated modern pop culture to the point where it is common for owners to use their NFTs as profile pictures on social media, or at least make posts about buying them. NFTs that are popularly used as profile pictures even have their own name, PFPs.

It is partly bragging rights as the owner does have something unique that can't technically be copied. A screenshot would not be the original, and would not mutate into other NFTs and can't be resold.

But could it extend further from pure narcissism?

As exemplified with Seth Green losing his NFT, not all NFTs are equal in security. However, those that implement technical best practices have built-in safety features – filing a report on the exchange the NFT was bought would usually enable the rightful owner the ability to deactivate the NFT, rendering it useless to whoever stole it. In addition, laws prohibit the sale of stolen goods including digital assets.

It is still very much the Wild West in crypto these days, and nothing is perfect, but the goal remains the same: NFTs will one day be a secure way to represent us online, as an avatar in the metaverse. Then, they would be as valuable as those coveted blue ticks on notable and trusted social media accounts. Or even part of the credentials a person carries around to participate in Barter 2.0.

But for now, it was the IP attached to Green's Bored Ape NFT that made him pay US$300 000 to get it back from a person who bought the NFT after it was discreetly resold on an exchange. NFTs do not always carry IP rights, but in Bored Ape's case, they do. Green had planned to have his NFT adapted into a starring role for an animation-live action show about a bartending monkey named Fred Simian.

When the token was stolen, however, existing copyright laws meant the *Family Guy* star lost his commercial rights to the ape character.

It is clear that security and market regulation needs to be tightened for NFTs before they can reach the next step, but influential people and companies as well as governments, are already looking into how NFTs can expand their brands' online presence and replace legacy systems like ballot voting.

It is highly plausible that future elections will be run using NFTs as ballots. Politicians are currently minting NFTs containing their videos to sway younger voters and get people to engage with their candidates. And supporters see it as more bang for their buck – something that might appreciate in value in return for their donations, which they would normally just give freely during rallies.

Governments want to restore the people's faith in the voting system as allegations of voting fraud continue and people demand more ease in the process to exercise their right to vote. Without the need to travel to vote, more people can take part in democracy and ruling regimes would not be able to hinder certain populations from the ballot boxes by force.

There are various communities and even Decentralized Autonomous Organizations (DAOs) that surround and support NFTs, creating communities where there is trust and a positive feedback loop to take projects, ideas, and agendas forward.

When Worlds Collide. . .

The hype that surrounds NFTs is no doubt compounded by the fact that many unscrupulous parties try to benefit off it by either scamming or resorting to gimmickry.

Just before this book was published, Mexican millionaire Martin Mobarak burned a rare US$10 million Frida Kahlo painting in a martini glass in front of a live audience at the NFT launch of the same artwork, shocking the art world and the whole country.

Mobarak defended his amazing display of arrogance by claiming that the proceeds of the 10 000 unique NFT copies of Kahlo's Fantasmones Sinistros, which was considered a cultural treasure by Mexico, would go to charity including to benefit the Palace of Fine Arts and the Frida Kahlo Museum.

If Mobarak genuinely wanted to contribute to society, he could have tied the NFTs to a percentage of ownership of the original physical artwork and incorporated more features down the line that would enable NFT holders to interact with the digital art world and real world, and even provide them with exclusive access to gallery openings that benefit the artist's foundations. Instead, what he did was simply the destruction of priceless art to guarantee demand for 10 000 replicas minted by his own company.

You could dismiss Mobarak's actions as that of a selfish businessman, he is a millionaire after all so he would naturally be concerned with profit. However, even internationally acclaimed artists are jumping on the bandwagon.

Just a month before the burning of the Frida Kahlo painting, British artist Damien Hirst told buyers who bought pieces from his latest collection to choose to keep either the physical artwork or the NFT representing it. He then proceeded to burn the physical pieces for buyers who chose the NFTs. When asked how he felt about burning his works, Hirst said, "It feels good, better than I expected."

Works burned by Hirst are estimated to total almost £10 million in value. It is Hirst's first NFT collection. Named "The Currency," 10 000 NFTs were sold for £1800 each, corresponding to 10 000 unique physical pieces of art. Some 5149 buyers went for the physical artworks while 4851 chose their corresponding NFTs.

Boisterous acts like Mobarak's and Hirst's stunts need to be countered by facts, use cases, and a reiteration of decentralized finance (DeFi)'s vision of creating an inclusive decentralized Web 3.0 digital economy.

Use cases are particularly important. The more use cases we have, the more value and trust we build. It is particularly important how NFTs evolve from here on – dynamic NFTs are the way forward.

Considered technically superior over static NFTs, dynamic NFTs are more flexible and expand the possible use cases of NFTs, connecting the digital asset to the real world.

Metadata does not change in static NFTs. Dynamic NFTs, however, allow metadata to be altered using smart contracts. This enables the digital asset to evolve in ways never thought possible before as real-world data interacts with it.

Smart contracts configured at the minting stage will determine the rules for the evolution of dynamic NFTs. And real-world data can be a factor in how your NFT changes. Oracles, which provide a link between real-world events and digital contracts, are now a common feature in smart contracts. This means off-chain data from sources such as web API and IoT data could be accessed to influence the growth of dynamic NFTs.

Although the gaming world already has digital assets that can be upgraded or leveled-up on their respective platforms, there is currently no portability between games and with the real world. With dynamic NFTs and AR, something a gamer does in real life could affect their digital asset in a game while art piece NFTs could change with the weather.

Currently, use cases are being developed for dynamic NFTs tied to personalities in the real world who are already using their performance and fame to determine their financial ranking. Musicians, celebrities, and athletes are just some of these people.

Let's take a closer look at a few dynamic NFTs around today.

LaMelo Ball is one of the pioneering dynamic NFT projects around. What makes this NFT project different is that the NFT of the NBA's Rookie of the Year is tied to his stats. This means the more Ball's career advances in the NBA, the more valuable his rookie NFTs get.

As digital collectibles, the NFTs level-up and evolve based on Ball's real-world performance. When he won Rookie of the Year in the 2020–2021 NBA season, the NFT changed its color to gold, and the planet Saturn that he was holding metamorphosed into the sun.

Source: NFT Stats https://www.nft-stats.com/collection/lamelo-ball-collectibles

Mike Tyson is creating his own gaming metaverse: an alien world built by the likes of former designers from Wargaming, Ubisoft, Blizzard, and Pixar. Part of the game's lore revolves around pigeons – Tyson's favorite animal – that are represented as dynamic NFTs that the metaverse users can use for gameplay in the Web 3.0 based trading card game Final Form. Some 10 000 trading card-like NFTs called Iron Pigeons were made available in a free mint for users.

In P2E (play-to-earn) games, Chainlink Verifiable Randomness Function (VFR) – part of blockchain technology – allows random distribution of traits and in-game items to determine the rarity of digital assets. Because it is built on-chain, the random results are verifiable and invulnerable to any attempts at manipulation. What BAYC and CryptoKitties revealed is just the beginning as games break away from their vertical axis and cross-game, cross-platform play becomes more of the norm.

DJ Steve Aoki, who said he's made more money on NFTs than his music, launched his own series of collectible NFTs that feature clips from the upcoming stop-motion series *Dominion X*. Using interactive Ether Cards Dynamic NFT technology, fans can own a piece of a show, both physical and digital, before it premieres on television or streaming platforms. In addition, the NFT investor has other plans to use dynamic NFTs to connect with his fans. Aoki said, "I think that the logical progression of where NFTs are going is a deeper and interactive experience between creators and fans facilitated by attaching real-world utility to NFTs."

All three examples above use Ether Cards to bring their NFTs to life.

Ether Cards is one of the leading NFT gamification and monetization platforms that connects real-world utility with the digital world, allowing personalities like

Aoki, Tyson, Ball, and the NBA to connect with their communities in engaging ways, while unlocking new monetization channels.

NFTs take up the lion's share of the digital assets market today, and it is only a matter of time until all NFTs become dynamic NFTs. But for this to happen, the metaverse has to be further developed and NFTs have to build more use cases. The gaming industry is the best place to do this.

Dynamic NFTs can come in the form of skins that evolve with the player's health, weapon upgrades that get better when players improve their stats – anything that is able to move out of an e-wallet and into the metaverse would be possible as an NFT in the future. Portability is guaranteed as long as the games are built on the same blockchain. In this aspect, games will evolve so that assets are portable across games.

Games test skills and NFTs will increase in value if assets give players an edge. NFTs can be staked like in lootbox matches where the winner takes all, or in more formal competitive settings. A new gaming economy could emerge where gamers can commoditize their digital assets and time spent playing games going beyond the already multibillion dollar e-sports industry.

Once it becomes the norm for games to be on the metaverse, e-sports trophies will come in the form of NFTs, where they will carry value and can be used as a form of crowdsourcing for future tournaments.

Reputation tokens that will be used as credentials in the Web 3.0 economy could also potentially be special NFTs awarded by decentralized community members to police behavior and encourage more ethical engagement and gameplay.

Since crypto can only exist in regulated exchanges as a currency, NFTs are seen as blockchain-powered consumer products. And these products need a space to call home, whether they are still on-sale on digital racks in digital malls or already bought and ready for display and use in digital homes.

Which brings us to where all marketplaces, companies, banks, personalities, governments, and people will meet to interact and have economic activity in the future: the metaverse.

A Meaningful Place

Believe it or not, the most popular game among 5–12 years old in the United States is not one game in particular, but a gaming platform that offers thousands of games from a variety of genres created by the users themselves.

Roblox is an online game platform and game creation system developed by Roblox Corporation that allows users to program games and play games created by other users, and it brings in big bucks although it is completely free to make a Roblox account. The game

beat Fortnite in the United Kingdom in terms of
in-game spending and the company that owns Roblox
recently began trading on the New York Stock
Exchange, valued at a staggering US$45 billion.

Source: Roblox Corporation

The in-game currency used is Robux, which can be
purchased with real money. Game developers get paid a
percentage of the subscription fee from premium users
based on how much time players spend in their
virtual worlds and when users purchase in-game
products – anyone can buy clothes to dress up their
avatars directly from the games on the platform, but
only premium membership users can sell them. If an
item has limited edition status, it can only be traded
between or sold by users with a Roblox Premium
membership. The highest earning game creators on this
platform make over US$100 000 annually on sales of
in-game items.

Released in 2006, the platform hosts user-created games coded in the programming language Lua. It had been relatively quiet for Roblox until the second half of the 2010s, when investors started taking note of its potential. In 2020, the game platform's popularity exploded due to the COVID-19 pandemic causing worldwide lockdowns.

Playable on-the-go, Roblox can be accessed on various devices, from XBox to phone to laptop. The platform has more than 32.6 million daily users with 8 million active creators and developers from 180 countries creating the games. Many creators on the platform have turned their hobby into a full-time job, with the developer community estimated to have earned around US$250 million in 2020.

The sheer number of game creators in this rudimentary metaverse as well as its friendly user interface to create games is a sign of what is to come.

Mobile gaming, wearable VR, AR, e-sports, online multiplayer settings, cloud gaming, and an ever-growing legion of fans ensure the continued growth of the gaming industry. Being accustomed to paying for upgrades to their characters and customizable skins to make their appearances unique, the adoption of digital assets or NFTs that complements the gaming experience in metaverses is inevitable.

Gamers represent various segments of the market and there are millions of us around the globe. They are the perfect test subjects and highest potential adopters of in-game currency and other digital assets based on supply and demand. It has already happened in Web 2.0, where digital assets were sold out of their gaming platforms on online marketplaces like Alibaba or Shopee, albeit crudely by the transferring of accounts, which carries a high risk of scams.

The gaming economy is prime to reach the next level where it transforms into a marketplace that allows trading of digital assets with real-world assets. My upgraded, one-of-a-kind Call of Duty sniper rifle in exchange for your outgoing iPhone perhaps? Gamers in countries currently heavily sanctioned with trade embargoes would jump at the opportunity.

Even if a gamer did not buy the digital asset but acquired it through gameplay – like if it was awarded to the gamer for completing certain tasks or side-quests – the merit-based gaming item could still be sold. After all, time equals money and that is what all gamers put in. This makes it all the more competitive and rewarding for serious gamers, while being inclusive toward newbies. Competitive gamers will see financial opportunities beyond winning championships, leading to the birth of in-game entrepreneur-gamers that will coincide with the adoption of metaverse marketplaces by traditional merchants.

Open-world games are a vivid representation of what can be achieved visually in the metaverse. By far, these games have been the top performers in sales for the past 20 years or so. Metaverse gaming open worlds are likely to be multiplayer, multi-server on a significantly larger scale than what gamers experience presently, and with blockchain integration, and all games would be linked to players' wallets.

Players competing with each other creates a digital GDP. From here, the use cases can be adapted to non-gaming interactions in the metaverse, from trading to services.

If the aim is a decentralized Web 3.0, much like how the early internet was envisioned to be before central powers took over, metaverse regulations will be determined by DAOs and voting by users. Every interaction will be evaluated and ranked, and handing out Reputation Tokens will be a common right for digital citizens. Economic activity in the metaverse will take precedence when it comes to enforcement of appropriate behavior.

Forecasts for the metaverse have been bright and sunny. Major corporations all over the world are buying digital land from metaverse developers such as Decentraland and Sandbox.

With smart contracts validating ownership, more online transactions will enter the metaverse, adding to our virtual experience, and birthing the worldwide 24/7 digital economy. Games today are just the nexus or precursor to it all, and non-gaming companies have noted the benefits.

As AI gets better, it will become a part of our daily lives. Companies will capitalize on AI technology as they continue to invest in the metaverse before the public adopts it. As rationalized in JP Morgan's report, the cost of investment is still relatively low compared to the benefits of having a stake in a plot of virtual land to awe customers in the future with products and services showcased in a fully developed Web 3.0 metaverse.

A recent example, Maxis, one of the leaders in a consortium of telcos bringing 5G to Malaysia, announced the Maxis Centre Decentraland – a virtual telco store where users will be able to purchase products and services with 3D technology, simulate how they could transform their homes with devices and appliances powered by 5G, and purchase collectible NFTs produced in collaboration with Malaysian artists, among other innovations.

Eventually, the metaverse will encompass the rest of the world as more big businesses and banks enter it, and governments launch their own Central Bank Digital Currencies (CBDCs) running on the blockchain.

Customer service could come in the form of non-playable characters (NPC) who get better at understanding customers as more interaction and data is collected. This creates more meaningful economic activity, which is part of the vision that the DeFi movement wants realized.

Economic activity is a series of actions that creates a transaction, not just the transaction itself. It is everything we do before and after the transaction. Dynamic NFTs allow pre- and post-data to be included inside these transactions.

Meaningful economic transactions happen when the evolving data they carry have records that are trustable. This is why everyone, from conglomerates to governments, wants your data. With data, what is unsellable today can be tweaked and turned into the sales-hit of tomorrow. Data is the new goal of the global economy.

NFTs and crypto are just representations of that data's worth. A unique code that ties ownership to smart contracts on-chain. Whether a picture of an ape that you can use as your profile, or an asset that is linked to real-world behavior, you should always know what you are buying into because it just might be a piece of the future that we can't recognize for now.

9 Of Builders and Villains. . .

For ardent critics of decentralized finance (DeFi), cryptocurrency is frowned upon as fool's gold, and it is not hard to see why. Drawn by the attractiveness of high returns, investors literally throw their life savings in crypto without any prior research into the risks surrounding digital currencies and lose everything in some cases.

A nonsensical, Ponzi scheme of an investment with no real value backing it, which just looks good because of prospects and hype: fool's gold.

But little do we know that the old adage that was coined during gold rushes of the past was originally meant to refer to other forms of metals and minerals that were mistaken for the precious metal at the time. The three main culprits are pyrite, chalcopyrite, and weathered mica. They are shiny and have industrial use cases but hold nowhere near the value of gold.

Likewise, the fool's gold that critics refer to in crypto are projects covered with smokescreens hiding their true balance sheets. And there are plenty of these threatening to destroy what the DeFi movement has worked so hard to build over the past decade and a half.

Cryptocurrency was meant to bank the unbankable, not create another gold rush, although that seems to be inevitable with today's unceasing flow of information and misinformation driven by social media content. Cryptocurrency is literally referred to as "digital gold" by both well-versed financial industry players as well as social media influencers who know little to nothing about what they are investing millions in or promoting. So it is naturally confusing for anyone who wants to venture into this new territory. What more for the man on the street who doesn't understand blockchain terminology or how the economy works?

Because of all the hype and aping going around, some retail investors are not prepared when markets take a dip, make a correction, or downright crash. On the flipside, they are more than willing to follow the crowd when things are bright and shiny. Billions of dollars have been lost as a result of poor due diligence, as well as homes seized by creditors and lives wrecked – people do not deserve this even if they are gullible.

The public does not deserve to be duped by villains who are really just bad actors masquerading as legit among committed builders who are working to create value-based blockchain ecosystems. And if you think that only ignorant retail investors have been victims, think again.

Government-owned traditional financial institutions and giant private hedge funds, with all their experts armed with their analytical and technical chart readings and predictions, were not immune to the lemming effect. This effectively means that even though you haven't placed a single cent into any crypto token or project, some pension fund, bank, or state-run financial institution that manages your money, did.

The fall of Terra (LUNA) and FTX, which brought down the whole cryptocurrency industry along with them, showed that even reliable institutions that are entrusted with state capital can make mistakes. However, what regular people don't have are large reserves to continue trading to cover losses from erroneous buy calls. For many, this would be the end of the road.

With both LUNA and FTX's crashes making headlines, it is hard to ignore the negative backlash and distrust that they have brought onto the industry. Those were not ordinary crashes caused by FUD (fear, uncertainty, doubt), like we've seen before when China banned crypto or when a big exchange gets hacked, like in 2014 with Mt. Gox. Even the pandemic did not cause this much damage to crypto markets.

In 2019, LUNA launched at US$1.31. After a dismal first 18 months, LUNA started to climb and hit its peak of US$119.18 in April 2022. Barely a month later, things started to go downhill.

The original LUNA market cap was about US$41 billion and was alleged to be backed by US$3.5 billion in Bitcoin reserves in the event of a major incident. This would make the company one of the top 10 BTC holders. But in May 2022, that market cap fell to below US$1 billion.

The project's related "stablecoin" TerraUSD (UST) boasted a 20% yield for investors who stored their coins in the system. Like Binance, investors are able to stake their owned crypto and receive deposit yield. This works like how traditional banks pay you an interest for keeping your money with them. TerraUSD's highly attractive yield, which was way better than interest you'd get from cash deposits at traditional banks, and LUNA's short and wild rise to its peak price were what attracted many investors.

As of 3 December 2022, the price of LUNA sits at US$0.000 182 – a massive fall that can be calculated in a variety of ways to paint a picture as grievous as any seen in the history of wartime hyperinflation.

Both LUNA and the "algorithmic stablecoin" TerraUSD that LUNA is meant to stabilize by being minted and burned according to supply and demand are the brainchild of Singapore-based Terraform Labs, which was co-founded by South Korean CEO Do Kwon.

Listed in *Asia Forbes'* "30 Under 30" list in 2019, Do Kwon's arrogant social media persona and constant flaming of rival blockchain projects gained him notoriety in the industry. However, he was still able to earn the trust of veteran fund managers and leading e-commerce players, until over US$45 billion was lost by his company in less than a week.

FTX, which started and crashed around the same time as LUNA, was the world's second-largest crypto exchange at one point. The company's CEO Sam Bankman-Fried, or SBF, became known as a philanthropic billionaire – one popular YouTuber labeled him as the "World's Most Generous Billionaire." His net worth, in just two short years, reached a whopping US$26 billion. SBF rubbed shoulders with Jeff Bezos and numerous celebrities, while big financial institutions like BlackRock, SoftBank, and Temasek invested in FTX. But while praised for his confidence (he made a multi-billion-dollar deal over the phone while playing *League of Legends*), the 30 year old was actually running the exchange's operations out of the Bahamas with a small group of friends.

It has been nothing short of one of the greatest swindles in the cryptocurrency space thus far, complete with bizarre amphetamine-fueled rantings of sister company Alameda Research CEO Caroline Ellison and amorous relationships between the group of crypto kids that ran the show.

Some US$51 billion was lost in the company's collapse. It is highly likely we will see a Netflix documentary on FTX in the near future. Collectively, both FTX and LUNA crashes wiped out over US$500 billion in the global crypto market.

Critics of DeFi have been up in arms ever since the fall of these two giants. Some even pointed out that the fall this time was caused by the very same thing that DeFi was trying to oppose: the unscrupulous practices and deceit used by bankers in the United States that caused the Global Financial Crisis of 2007–2008.

It is not worth asking if crypto will ever recover to the highs it reached in November 2021 if we can't look into the mirror and ask ourselves, "Am I just following a crowd that is following a villain?" FTX and LUNA are the lessons we need to learn before we move on. They have become DeFi's Day of Reckoning.

Let's prevent the same from happening again by taking a closer look at both of these bad actors. . .

Walking on the Moon: The Rise and Fall of Terra LUNA

The idea was to create a price-stable crypto payment system backed by the biggest e-commerce platforms. It was an idea that was worth exploring at the time, but it did not go beyond that: an idea. Not until investors started pouring in and exposed the flaws of the system that turned out to be a smartly concealed Ponzi scheme.

Usually, stablecoins are backed by real-world assets, mainly with fiat USD itself, and have a cap or limit based on their reserves. But TerraUSD (UST) is different. It is an "algorithmic stablecoin" that worked based on another digital currency called LUNA, which would be minted and burned to stabilize the price of UST.

Stablecoins are seen by investors as a safer alternative to the unpredictable fluctuations of cryptocurrencies. The goal of stablecoins is to provide a fixed 1:1 exchange rate with the dollar or any other currency it sets out to be pegged to. This is not always the case; stablecoins do fall in value themselves, but there is seldom a significant difference. Prices might fall to US$0.94–0.98, and a dip to US$0.90 will trigger some selling pressure. However, no stablecoin has tanked as much as UST, which is now only worth around US$0.019, or over 98% down from its initial price.

LUNA did not have any other reason to exist besides its function of stabilizing UST. It was the smokescreen disguised as the system itself. A widget that is bought and sold to create USD value for UST. It is preposterous as it was unnecessary. If there were no real-world assets backing one digital currency (UST), then using another (LUNA) to generate that was extremely suspicious.

To give the illusion that LUNA had value besides being a stabilizer for UST, investors were offered a mouth-watering 20% yield for deposits, beating traditional banks by a significant amount and attracting many ordinary folk who were just getting started in crypto and ironically thought that this would be a safer alternative. The magical yield that appeared out of nowhere soon took precedence over the original idea to be a price-stable e-commerce currency. Greed took over and won.

But no one should take the blame more than co-founder and CEO Do Kwon.

The Terra Network was launched by Do Kwon and Daniel Shin in January 2018 with the goal to create an e-commerce payments application called Chai, which would have its own price-stable crypto. They were looking to take on the likes of Alipay and Paypal, and with the volatility of other cryptocurrencies making it hard for crypto to be used as everyday currency, their currency had to be branded as a "stablecoin."

Eventually, Terraform Labs was created in April 2018 in Singapore, and with it, LUNA and UST were born, supported by the Terra Alliance – a consortium of 15 Asian large e-commerce companies.

It is noteworthy that they chose Singapore, a country known for its strict regulations on financial products, as its headquarters. The move definitely gave the company a more trustworthy appearance.

However, according to insiders who spilled the beans to crypto-related media such as ColdFusionTV, Do Kwon was a control freak who was as narcissistic as he was charismatic, often berating his employees to the point that most of the core team left on a bitter note after a year or two, with legal suits filed against him.

One thing is evident from his Twitter feed: Do Kwon was not only fond of criticizing other blockchain projects, which made him a dark horse, but also not respected among builders in the community.

Other crypto experts, like MakerDAO's head of risk Cyrus Younessi, voiced their concerns early in the project's inception. As a former research analyst at Scaler, he explained to his former employer why UST and LUNA did not make sense and gave a doomsday scenario that came true about four years later.

Nevertheless, a year later, in January 2019, LUNA's initial coin offering (ICO) saw early investors going in at US$0.18 per token during its seed round, and US$0.80 per token at a private sale. A flimsy white paper called Terra Money, written by Do Kwon and several other co-authors, followed in April 2019. White papers should always come before any ICO.

Fast forward a year later, in 2020, LUNA now has a staking product on a South Korean exchange. The Anchor protocol, a platform built on Terra, is announced soon after, allowing investors to earn a high yield on their deposits and borrow against their crypto holdings.

Deposit returns were guaranteed to be 20%. The news drove more retail investors as well as big institutions into the madness.

Terra blockchain's stablecoin, UST, came out later that year with its sights set on being launched on the Ethereum and Solana blockchains.

By December 2021, LUNA's price was close to reaching its peak, now at above US$90. It seemed like LUNA really was digital gold when you think about a more than 90 times rise in value from just three years ago.

The following month, Do Kwan publicly denied the probability of an overload to the algorithm as the result of one massive pump-and-dump action on LUNA that would consequently cause a spiral in UST's value. There was still no cap to the limit of minting and burning of LUNA at this point.

To maintain UST's peg to the dollar, LUNA would keep minting, or so the logic went. It would work on small dips, but if UST's price fell too low and investors kept on selling, new LUNA tokens would continue to be minted to the point of hyperinflation.

This is not the case for normal cryptocurrencies like Bitcoin, Ether, or even altcoins that temporarily crash for a variety of reasons like panic selling or stop losses. Their supplies are fixed, meaning the amount of coins in circulation and those that are yet to be minted are finite and regulated. Crashes do not create or destroy these coins, hence, when markets recover so do the coins, as their intrinsic value and tech does not change.

As if to answer skeptics who questioned how the system could operate stably while paying out such a high yield, the Luna Foundation Guard was formed around this time with the aim to safeguard UST by building up reserves amid market volatility.

The foundation raised up to US$1 billion through the sale of LUNA tokens to buy Bitcoin to be used as UST reserves. Three Arrows Capital and Jump Crypto, two well-known trading and investment firms, walloped most of the offer.

On Twitter, influential crypto trader Algod called out UST and LUNA as a Ponzi scheme and bet US$1 million that the price of LUNA would be lower in a year. "Cool, I'm in" replied Do Kwon. Supporting Algod's claim, another trader who went by the handle GiganticRebirth raised the stakes and bet US$10million that LUNA would "pump short term" but in one year, the current narrative would be lost. Do Kwon agreed to match the stakes.

Setting crosshairs on MakerDAO and its token DAI, Do Kwon tweeted "By my hand $DAI will die" as he initiated a hostile takeover of the decentralized stablecoin's liquidity on decentralized crypto exchange Curve.

Declaring war on a well-known Decentralized Autonomous Organization (DAO) that created a respectable decentralized stablecoin did not sit well with most in the DeFi community, but a rift was already brewing in the stablecoin camp.

Allies of Do Kwon, companies with their own algorithmic stablecoins, grouped together to form liquidity cartels. They spoke about how overcollateralized stablecoins like DAI (which is backed by reserves of ETH and USDC) were taking a free ride on exchanges as they did not give back investors a yield that could compete with undercollateralized stablecoins.

The Luna Foundation Guard went on to bag an alleged US$3.5 billion in BTC reserves, making it one of the top 10 bitcoin holders in the world. For a while, it seemed like UST and LUNA would emerge as the dominant stablecoins in the market.

Despite the clear and present danger sounded by others in the community, the project was able to raise more capital and investors were happy. When LUNA's price hit its all-time high of US$119.2 on 5 April 2022, they were walking on the moon.

UST became the third largest stablecoin while Terra held the fourth largest market cap in the industry. The circulating supply of LUNA reached an all-time low of 346 million tokens as more LUNA tokens were burned to meet the demand for UST.

Because Do Kwon wanted a fixed 20% yield to entice investors, as opposed to paying a variable percentage based on the market, his company was paying out about US$7 million every day. Investors were also allowed to withdraw their deposits at any given time.

The risk of mass withdrawals, coupled with the high yield factor, was a recipe for exploitation and disaster.

Fanatic supporters of LUNA, who called themselves LUNATICS, ignored the simple possibility of a George Soros-style attack. Instead of stopping to think and adding more self-regulations, as one should as a member of the DeFi community, LUNATICS simply wanted Do Kwon to make them more money.

In an interview, when asked about how he views his competition, Do Kwon answered that 95% of them are going to die, adding that "there's also entertainment from watching companies die."

And then, the crash happened.

Leaked documents showing that Do Kwon filed to dissolve Terraform Labs days before UST and LUNA collapsed, managed to alert some investors, but not all.

A number of large dumps brought UST's price down to US$0.985. It is not a large dip as seen before with other stablecoins, which prompts Do Kwon to joke about the minor incident.

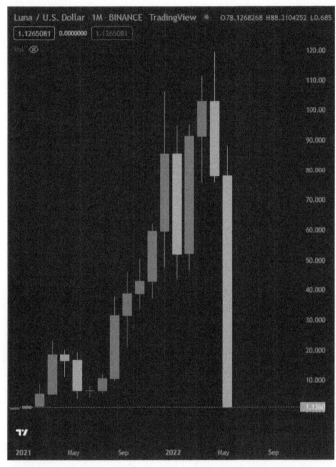

Source: Coindesk https://www.coindesk.com/layer2/2022/05/11/
the-luna-and-ust-crash-explained-in-5-charts/

From 9 May 2022 onward, UST went on a
downward spiral. When it reached US$0.92, the media
started taking note. A series of major withdrawals
followed that saw US$4 billion dumped. UST's 1:1 peg
to USD had clearly failed despite the company's
BTC reserves.

The Luna Foundation Guard announced a US$1.5 billion loan to rescue the peg, but overall, selling pressure maintained as the price fell below US$0.50. Meanwhile, LUNA hyperinflated and plunged further.

Do Kwon tweeted, "Deploying more capital – steady lads." More than half of traders on 11 May believed him and bought into LUNA, despite the drop a couple of days ago.

The next day, 12 May, LUNA's price fell by 96%.

In an attempt to save the peg, almost all of the Luna Foundation Guard's resources were depleted, in just a few days BTC reserves totaling around 80 000 BTC had been reduced to 313 BTC.

In the United States, regulators demanded an explanation for the crash from Do Kwon. One politician went as far as to call UST a modern-day pyramid scheme.

Source: Coindesk https://www.coindesk.com/layer2/2022/05/11/the-luna-and-ust-crash-explained-in-5-charts/

In Terraform Labs' defense, some have said that there are no signs of fraud committed on Do Kwon's part. However, it does not negate the fact that he knew that the Terra ecosystem could not sustain the rapid growth it was experiencing and that it was vulnerable to attacks.

Instead, Do Kwon was driven by greed himself and promised the heavens just to make his project grow. And it does not look like he has learned his lesson.

Later in the same month as the crash of UST (now worth around US$0.02) and LUNA (now only US$0.0 001 972 per token), a hard fork proposal was passed to rename Terra to Terra Classic (LUNC) and to launch a new Terra (LUNA) on a second blockchain.

However, in October 2022, the law came down on Do Kwon. As a South Korean national, authorities in the country wanted to have a word with him.

Rumored to be in Dubai at the moment, South Korean authorities are investigating him and his company under multiple charges including fraud and violation of the Capital Markets Act following the collapse of his project that caused a US$60 billion loss in crypto market capitalization.

The Seoul Southern District Prosecutors' Office issued an arrest warrant with passport nullification, and subsequently asked Interpol to launch a red notice on Kwon, which the agency passed. The red notice now allows global law enforcement to locate and arrest him.

From technopreneur to international criminal, Do Kwon's days might just be numbered now.

Good.

Sex, Drugs, and Balance Sheets: How a Bunch of Kids Created and Destroyed FTX

If there was ever a chance for Netflix to get in on some real-life drama involving the crypto world, this would be it and the documentary would start with one man, Sam Bankman-Fried (or SBF for short).

He was the CEO of FTX, the second largest crypto exchange in the world, trailing only behind Binance. SBF was also known as the most generous billionaire at one point in his short career. But all would come undone when he lost billions over a weekend.

SBF was born into a politically well-connected family. His father, a law professor, would later help his son to raise funds for his company.

After graduating from the Massachusetts Institute of Technology, SBF joined New York trading firm Jane Street Capital, where he would meet future members of FTX. Discovering a loophole where he could buy crypto in the United States and sell it in Japan for a higher price, SBF started shifting up to US$25 million a day.

With his profits, he started Alameda Research with some of his former college friends and Jane Street workmates. He suggested that Caroline Ellison, his former colleague, join Alameda in 2017. She would later go on to become the CEO of the company and be romantically involved with SBF.

Apparently, it was a thing in the company as a report in *Fortune* said that Alameda Research was "run by a gang of kids in the Bahamas" who all dated each other. The young group was known for partying hard, but Ellison herself would go on to publicly expose a disturbing personal trait on her Twitter account: admitting to being a regular and unabashed amphetamine user.

She would go to state on her Tumblr blog that she supports polygamous relationships with hierarchy and competition for lovers. Bizarrely comparing it to an "imperial Chinese harem" except with equality among genders, Ellison said "everyone should have a ranking of their partners, people should know where they fall on the ranking, and there should be vicious power struggles for the higher ranks."

Alameda Research was a crypto hedge fund that carried out trades, matched buyers and sellers, and supposedly gave investors a return. They promised 15% annualized fixed returns with no downside. As with LUNA's high yield, it was a magical number that appeared out of nowhere. And likewise, people bought it.

FTX, on the other hand, as SBF put it, was started because he saw that other crypto exchanges only catered to inexperienced traders. He wanted to give more options like futures and options trading for crypto, and tokenized stocks of real companies.

Both Alameda and FTX were based in the Bahamas and owned by SBF. Alameda Research later received US$10 billion in FTX customer funds without the knowledge or consent of customers, effectively a misuse of funds amounting to fraud.

SBF raised eyebrows when he managed to raise US$2 billion in funds for FTX, from various banks and investment companies including from BlackRock. According to a blog post from one of his major investors, venture capital firm Sequoia Capital, SBF was playing the game *League of Legends* when he closed a US$210 million deal with them.

SBF's ease of acquiring funds for his start-ups raised more questions regarding his politically connected family.

Nevertheless, crypto was rising at the time and things were going good for SBF. FTX was averaging US$10 billion a day in trades, breathing down the necks of rival exchange Binance.

SBF brought FTX to the world. In the United States, the company bought naming rights for sports stadiums. Ad campaigns starring the biggest celebrities were aired on TV. The celebrities were paid with FTX equity. Actor Tom Brady was reported to have put his US$650 million fortune into FTX to increase his equity.

In 2022, the United States was also ready to embrace its own Central Bank Digital Currency (CBDC), with government regulators and big banks backing the idea. SBF wanted FTX to be at the center of it.

As FTX became a household name, SBF became highly influential. The founder projected his life philosophy in Positive Altruism, which is basically all about finding the best version of yourself and what you can do to serve society. He wanted to appear as humble as possible to the world.

He chose to brand himself as a modest billionaire, choosing to drive a regular Toyota, to appear more trustworthy.

It was so convincing that even international governance lobbying groups were looking toward Sam for fresh ideas. FTX subsequently became a partner of the World Economic Forum and built the infrastructure for funds to reach Ukraine DAO amid the Russian invasion.

To gain political leverage, FTX had both sides of the coin in their pocket. SBF donated US$5 million to

Joe Biden in 2020, and a total of US$50 million to Democrat politicians ahead of the 2022 mid-term elections, whereas FTX co-CEO Ryan Salame donated US$23 million to Republican politicians.

However, even with a net worth of US$26 billion, SBF ran FTX mainly by himself and refused to form a Board of Directors. As founder of Alameda and FTX, he had the power to move assets around within both his companies.

In the second half of 2022, risk assets took a dive as the Fed raised interest rates to combat rising inflation. Cryptocurrencies were among the hardest hit. Alameda started making huge losses from trading and while trying to bailout companies it invested in.

SBF thought he could buy crypto at record low prices but did not count on reserves running out. But even before that happened, he cooked the books.

After Alameda lost money while trying to rescue crypto company Voyager from bankruptcy, Sam secretly moved at least US$4 billion from FTX to prop up Alameda's balance sheet. The currency he moved is in the form of FTT, which is FTX's native token.

FTT is FTX's own centrally controlled, printed out of thin air, token. And it generated most of the capital used to build FTX when it was sold to early investors.

Publicly, SBF stated it was just a routine involving "rotating a few FTX wallets" that are mostly non-circulating, adding that "we do this periodically" and it "won't have any effect."

It was the largest transfer of tokens on an exchange ever. People got suspicious. All these FTX wallets were technically transferring to just one recipient, which was a wallet at Alameda.

A probably tweaked out Ellison made matters worse when she slipped up during a call with a reporter from the *Wall Street Journal*, when she admitted that FTX used customers' monies to help Alameda resolve its liabilities.

On 2 November 2022, leaked documents revealed that most of Alameda's US$14.6 billion assets were in the form of FTT tokens. This meant that Alameda had close to nothing in its vault and had been trading with a potentially valueless currency: a fake token.

As the crypto market slid, the liquidity of FTT tokens fell. Suddenly, people were not as interested in FTT as when the token was going up in price and making them money.

In the early days of FTX, Binance founder-CEO Changpeng Zhao, commonly known as CZ, bought 20% of the company for US$100 million. SBF would later buy back the stock at US$2 billion, paid in FTT.

CZ's relationship with SBF began to sour as SBF quietly lobbied for a brokerage-like trading license in the United States that would effectively give FTX an edge over all of its competition. Binance, being the largest exchange and biggest rival to FTX, would lose out the most.

The political connections in SBF's family, as well as Caroline's family, began to emerge. It has been reported that Gary Gensler, Head of the Securities & Exchange Commission (SEC) and Caroline's father Glenn Ellison, both worked at MIT as professors. The senior Ellison was Gensler's boss.

Another alleged leaked email suggests that the SEC gave FTX a conditional "no action relief" and looked the other way when faced with claims that FTT was being used to deceive investors.

CZ, at the revelation of the leaked documents, knew he had the power to bring down FTX with the US$2 billion worth of FTT.

On 6 November, less than a week after the leaked documents revealed FTT's true form, CZ tweeted that Binance would liquidate all FTT tokens on their books. Effectively mass dumping FTT on the open market "due to recent revelations."

SBF went on the defense and tweeted: "A competitor is trying to go after us with false rumors. FTX is fine. Assets are fine." However, in correspondence with staff, SBF admitted that a giant withdrawal surge was happening and that six billion tokens were withdrawn in the last 72 hours.

SBF tried to keep his cool. "Obviously, Binance is going after us. So be it," he reportedly told staff. FTT went down 80% over the next two days, depleting FTX reserves even further.

FTX had US$9 billion in liability and only US$900 million in liquid assets. This meant they could not pay out all of the withdrawals.

As a final effort to glue their house of cards from falling apart, Ellison tweeted to CZ offering to buy up Binance's FTT holdings. "Alameda will happily buy it all from you today at $22!"

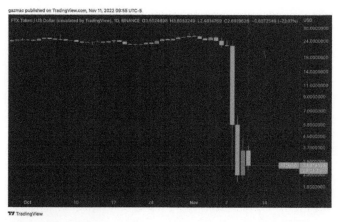

Source: Bloomberg https://www.bloomberg.com/opinion/articles/ 2022-11-11/ftx-collapse-don-t-start-dancing-on-crypto-s-grave- just-yet

CZ replied, "Liquidating our FTT is just post-exit risk management, learning from LUNA. We gave support before, but we won't pretend to make love after divorce. . . we won't support people who lobby against other industry players behind their backs."

Following this, SBF called CZ to offer FTX up for sale. CZ agreed to buy FTX "to save them," but in reality, he was consolidating power by buying up FTX at an extremely discounted price. Once CZ got a chance to look into FTX's books however, the deal was off.

FTX's gap between liabilities and assets was underestimated by everyone, coming short of a reported US$8 billion. Soon, the US Department of Justice began to investigate the US$10 billion of FTX customers' funds that were mysteriously channeled into Alameda.

With no liquidity and resources, FTX was forced to stop withdrawals. On 11 November, FTX and Alameda filed for bankruptcy. The news shocked the market and erased more than US$152 billion in three days. The exchange, valued at US$32 billion earlier in the year, was wiped off the face of the earth, leaving a permanent scar on the whole crypto market. How could things have changed so fast?

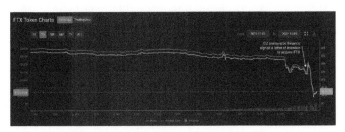

Source: Coindesk https://mishtalk.com/economics/ crypto-crash-is-led-by-a-whopping-88-percent-plunge-in-ftx

FTX had a web of investments and acquisitions, mainly brokered with FTT. The crash of FTX affected overall investor confidence in crypto, waves of retail and institutional investors left. Many projects that received FTX support in the form of FTT went into bankruptcy as well.

If this wasn't enough, it was discovered that US$1 billion of customers' money that was transferred to Alameda had vanished.

And then FTX got hacked!

As though the fall from grace had not ended, FTX claimed that a hacker drained whatever remained of their funds which sat at around US$600 million in crypto. Many customers who still had access to the platform despite its legal and financial woes, started noticing that their balances were now showing zero.

Write downs from institutions followed. SoftBank wrote down nearly US$100 million, its former COO expressing regret and cited FOMO for the blunder. Singapore's Temasek wrote down US$275 million in addition to its reputational damage. Hedge fund Galois Capital, which was among the few that spotted the crash of LUNA before it happened, still has half of its capital trapped in FTX, while the Ontario Teachers' Pension Plan had US$95 million stuck in FTX during the crash.

Collective liabilities, including that of all affiliated companies of FTX, are estimated to be US$50 billion.

Sam is currently under house arrest in the Bahamas. Once carrying a net worth of US$26 billion, SBF was now worth a negative sum.

US officials are now in talks with the Bahamian government to extradite SBF to the United States for trial, so we might just see some justice served. Whether the missing funds will be found is another story.

Speculation, the Language of Fools

The ICO boom from 2017 to 2022 saw a lot of new players entering the crypto world. While we welcome the enthusiastic arrival of new brethren DeFi projects, we have to watch out for the wolves in sheep's clothing.

The irony is that both Terra LUNA and FTX started out with good intentions, but greed and hubris took them in a different direction.

Stablecoins have a use and it was to offer people a chance to avoid the volatility of crypto, while properly managed exchanges are essential to bring crypto to a wider world.

However, Do Kwon and SBF turned out to be bad actors in a bull market. A lot of innocent people were hurt and even the DeFi community was divided.

There are a lot of similarities between these two cases, one striking point is that Do Kwon and SBF acted as central powers within their own projects. Even though they worked in small teams, there was little to no democracy, and a lot of intimidation tactics. They were unscrupulous dictators digging their own graves.

Like the traders who called out LUNA before it crashed, the community needs to come together to heighten our knowledge-sharing and call out villains or bad actors. We need to stop them before they are able to launch their projects and swindle more money. We need to shame them for the damage to the reputation of DeFi.

As the whole crypto industry is driven by speculative value, the crash of FTX and LUNA is a wake-up call for us to embrace utility value. Utility is what will separate the real cryptos from the fakes. Currency only has value when it has use.

The more we realize what value really is, the faster we will conclude that it does not always have to be in the form of traditional money. Payment solutions do not necessarily have to be limited to an amount of dollars for a day's work.

This is why there are some who are more bullish on seeing DeFi work in the gaming and entertainment industries rather than in the financial realm. Sometimes, seeing is believing, as with non-fungible token (NFT) where utility is tangible and expandable in countless ways.

People will always want to play good games and have quality entertainment even when the market is down. The utility from NFTs can transcend market sentiments and set a precedent for the adoption of crypto later on. Crypto should never be invented as just a means to an end. All blockchain projects must have a mission statement; a token cannot just be there to serve or stabilize another coin.

A blockchain's mission statement shapes its utility. Investors should only go into projects that bring intrinsic value to the real world.

Moving forward, we need more regulation and due diligence for higher standards of trading, especially with venture capitalists and hedge funds as they can influence the market. At the end of the day, it is the retailers who follow these big institutions that get hurt the most.

Self-policing the DeFi community means that we all have to play our part in identifying the Builders from the Villains. The largest blockchain needs to come together as soon as possible to form consortiums to set up watchdogs and regulators.

If we wait for regulators or the government to step in, it would be too late. We cannot afford the reputational damage that future bad actors might wreak. It is better for us to set ourselves straight, have each other's backs, and stay vigilant.

The joyride is over, please fasten your seatbelts.

And remember, not all that glitters is gold.

10 The Nature of a Nurturer: Reflecting on the Klaytn Journey

I have always been a person who has enjoyed setting up or growing ecosystems in the blockchain/crypto space. A lot of my friends in the industry describe me as a "zero to one" kind of guy. So, when I was asked in early 2021 to meet with one of the Co-Founders and Vice Chairman of Kakao Group to discuss an opportunity to join Klaytn (Kakao's blockchain), to help globalize the platform, I was thrilled. For those of you who don't know Kakao, the simplest way to explain it is that it's Korea's version of WeChat. Over 95% of the population has a KakaoTalk account. KakaoTalk was their first product that they created and the first chat application to have a group chat feature. Subsequently, off the back of their success in launching what is now technically Korea's national communication app, they started to expand their platform business into other areas like gaming, entertainment, ride-hailing, internet banking, and Web3/blockchain.

It was an absolute honor and pleasure to have been asked to take the role as Head of Global Adoption at Klaytn. Consequently, with the growth of the team and expanded responsibilities, I took on an expanded mandate of Global Group Head, which was my last official title before leaving Klaytn in December 2022. For a year and half, I put all my energy and effort in pulling together a global strategy, team, and structure that would help Klaytn go from an obscure local Korean blockchain project to a globally recognized and prized platform for Developers, Investors, and Partners to want to be a part of. By far it was the biggest challenge that I had faced up to that point in my career. To build international momentum around a project that was really only known to Koreans onshore while restructuring the identity of Klaytn from a decentralized finance (DeFi) centric ecosystem to a blockchain focused on the metaverse, gaming, and the creator economy, this was a tall task that required a lot more than the traditional resources needed to build up and scale a Layer 1 blockchain.

It was around August–September 2021 and I remember having some anxiety leading up to a big presentation I was asked to make, where the whole organization was waiting to hear my view on Klaytn's new global plan. Korean users and Klaytn have generally been more "DeFi" centric and less geared to "Web3" projects which can be associated with use cases such as gaming or entertainment. This meant that there were historically more projects that were building DeFi trading infrastructure on Klaytn than for instance games or non-fungible token (NFT)-driven applications. To convince the organization that we would be making a complete shift was not only a tall order but also a risky proposition if it didn't work out. At that time, I recall that one of the largest projects on Klaytn was a platform called Klayswap, a DeFi application. By the time I left, one of the growing projects on Klaytn in addition to Klayswap was a game called DeFi Kingdoms. This is relevant as DeFi Kingdoms is a prime example in representing the transformation that the global team led which ultimately attracted such a large US-based project to migrate their game to Klaytn from a competitor.

The competition for onboarding good projects in the blockchain industry is fierce. There is a lot of work in attributing the right resources and focus to bring projects in and to ensure that they see success. One critical resource is marketing. When I joined Klaytn there was no real marketing team. This was a function that I've always said is as important if not more important than the engineering function. As a blockchain ecosystem, it is imperative to be able to have channels on social media, at physical events, traditional media outlets, and other communication platforms (Telegram, Discord, etc.), so that communities are engaged and announcements can be amplified. It was a priority for me to have the right marketing capabilities in place on Day 1 to ensure a proper echo chamber was created which was necessary to increase the global adoption of Klaytn. Consequently, one of the earliest things that I did was to convince the decision makers at Klaytn in Korea that we needed marketing to be done out of Singapore and not onshore in Korea. With their blessing, I started to build a team in Singapore as a launch pad for developing marketing strategies such as community management, event management, growth, communication management, thought leadership advocacy, and developer relations. All these key components were necessary in getting Klaytn to a competitive space to be able to compete with the likes of other large global blockchain projects.

Finally, one other function that was important to the global strategy was to internationalize the voice of

the Klaytn engineers which were predominantly native
Korean speakers prior to my arrival. If we wanted to be
global, we needed to ensure we had the right level of
cultural diversity with developer/engineering support
representing all the different regions that we wanted to
be part of. So, I created the Ecosystem Development
(Eco Dev) team which was a subset of the Core
Developers that Klaytn had within the engineering
group. The idea was that I would build the Eco Dev
team and then hand the team off to the Head of the
Core Developer group once all the relevant hires were
made and the structure was set. It was natural for me to
lean on my history with people that I met in my
10-year journey in crypto/blockchain to find the right
people to trust with this key function. It took an
American engineer living in Korea and a Hong Kong
engineer living in the United Kingdom to set the
wheels in motion as the two leads to build the Eco Dev
team around. The team continues to be a critical
function in the Klaytn ecosystem supporting projects
and leading developer advocacy while expanding the
onboarding journey into Klaytn and increasing
developer awareness globally.

As I reflect on my time and impact on Klaytn as an
organization and an ecosystem, I'm proud of all those
who worked alongside me, joining me in the journey
and trusting me to lead them. It was a privilege and an
honor working with some of the most talented people

in the Web3 space that I was lucky enough to convince to join the ride. In addition, the motivation that I personally had to fulfill a promise made to the Vice Chairman of the Kakao Group ended up being a key driver for me to push even as the industry was going through a bear market, mounds of volatility, and many, many internal obstacles and challenges along the way. Looking back at my time with Klaytn, it was truly the global team that led the overall organization to see that it is possible to compete for and win large global projects like DeFi Kingdoms and that pivoting away from trading-based speculative use cases to a more diverse utility-based environment was ultimately the right thing to do.

A Blockchain to Connect All Blockchains

There are at least a thousand blockchain projects in various stages of progress[1] and over 21 000 cryptos[2] in existence today. However inspiring that figure is, where we are right now is far from where we should be.

The industry has seen too many exponential ups and downs, most recently with the twin crashes of Terra

---

[1]How many blockchains are there in 2022? (Earthweb): https://earthweb.com/how-many-blockchains-are-there/
[2]How many cryptocurrencies are there in 2023? (Exploding Topics): https://explodingtopics.com/blog/number-of-cryptocurrencies

(Luna) and FTX that took down a huge chunk of the industry. Market volatility has led to the number of blockchain companies dropping from the year 2018 when there were 8112 blockchain companies to the 492 players that still stand in the first half of 2022.[3]

To clear the chaos, the Klaytn blockchain was created with the intention to nurture and scale new players in the market by providing the right tools to build and support metaverse and cryptocurrency ecosystems.

In 2019, Ground X, a subsidiary of the Kakao Group – one of South Korea's leading software enterprises – created the Klaytn blockchain as a scalable and user-friendly blockchain environment for decentralized applications (dApps) and services including metaverse gaming and gaming finance (GameFi), decentralized exchanges, marketplaces, and more. In total, the Klaytn ecosystem has 167 projects in these areas, including 52 centralized crypto exchanges (CEX) or payments protocols.

Klaytn offers builders a comprehensive package of tools and financial and managerial support including in-built Layer 2 solutions such as software development

---

[3]The number of newly founded blockchain companies is on a global decline in 2022 (GlobeNewswire): https://www .globenewswire.com/en/news-release/2022/09/27/2523292/0/ en/The-Number-of-Newly-Founded-Blockchain-Companies-is-on-a-Global-Decline-in-2022.html

kits (SDKs), wallets, oracles, chain explorers, bridges,
Decentralized Autonomous Organizations (DAOs),
and NFT marketplaces. By simplifying user interface,
Klaytn allows new developers to bypass complex
technology and get their projects moving.

**Klaytn offers end-to-end integration including
a built-in L2 solution**

Source: Klaytn Light Paper: https://klaytn.foundation/wp-content/
uploads/Lightpaper.pdf

The Ethereum blockchain is seen as the industry
standard; hence, Klaytn gives full attention to
Ethereum equivalence, ensuring that its system is
compatible and on-par with Ethereum's tech stack.
This way the Klaytn blockchain will benefit from
advancements made on Ethereum.

As an Ethereum Virtual Machine (EVM) Layer 1 blockchain, Klaytn is designed to be practical and reliable, focusing not just on technology and business but also on transformative change that will create public accessibility and a much-needed layer of trust in the age of Web3. All while providing a powerful infrastructure that is capable of processing more than 10 000 transactions-per-second (TPS) with just a few nodes, and with a gas fee that is lower than Ethereum's.

The Klaytn blockchain supports DeFi services including earning interest, borrowing, lending, and trading. BINANCE Staking and Kai Protocol operate on Klaytn and the chain has strategic partnerships with Netmarble, GMO Internet Group, and ConsenSys – whose popular Metamask wallet can be linked to the blockchain. As of January 2022, Klaytn has a total value locked (TVL) of US$172.14 million based on DeFiLama and is one of only eight blockchains integrated to OpenSea, the leading NFT marketplace.

Aside from investing in promising blockchain projects to grow the ecosystem and creating the infrastructure for the metaverse to interact with the real world, the Singapore-headquartered organization works tirelessly for sustainable global adoption.

After strengthening its internal processes, Klaytn is now set to move into its roadmap 2.0 phase which will

Source: Klaytn website: https://www.klaytn.foundation/
roadmap/

see exciting developments as it moves to include more
decentralization via increased governance by DAOs.

Klaytn 2.0 will also see more developer tools being
supported on the network including Witnet which
have integrated their oracle services onto the
blockchain.

The ecosystem will also add support for
applications in the form of investment funds,
performance incentives, treasury advisory, and
community building.

But to fully understand Klaytn's role in the next
step of Web3, we will have to take a closer look at what
makes it tick – from its technology to its governance.

TPS is King

Convenience will always be a determining factor in mass adoption. As such, Klaytn is dedicated to keeping its promise of having a one-second deterministic finality for all transactions. Settled quickly and irreversibly, it is consumer-friendly and secure.

Klaytn uses a hybrid consensus algorithm, a combination of Byzantine Fault Tolerance (BFT) and proof-of-stake (PoS), giving it high speed and efficiency while maintaining a high level of security.

BFT is used for initial block validation and PoS for final block confirmation. The duality of decentralized public blockchains and highly scalable private blockchains that is prevalent in Klaytn makes it a hybrid ecosystem, leveraging off the best of both worlds.

By customizing its own frameworks, such as the consensus algorithm called the Istanbul Byzantine Fault Tolerance (IBFT) framework, which is also used by Ethereum, the Klaytn blockchain is able to zip through processing transactions at lightning speed.

The IBFT contains three nodes that communicate with each other to verify and reach consensus. Consensus Nodes, Proxy Nodes, and Endpoint Nodes play unique roles in a block's generation and the synergy of the nodes enables consensus to be achieved quicker.

Klaytn's optimized version of the IBFT is able to process up to 4000 TPS with its one-second transaction finality, meaning it has the strength to be the foundation to the numerous Web3 projects that have been birthed on its platform, and heavy user transaction traffic.

Another growth factor is Klaytn's scaling through Service Chains. Called "spokes," Service Chains can be tailored for individual dApp requirements, and just like other Layer 2 solutions, "spokes" can be anchored to Klaytn's main chain for greater security. By building support for Service Chain bridging to enable seamless interoperability between participants in our ecosystem, the opportunity to size-up fast is abundant.

So far, Klaytn's "spokes" have been a great help in increasing efficiency. Eventually, the plan is to have nested Service Chains, allowing clusters of "spokes" to form as hubs for other Service Chains which could mean exponential growth in scalability.

TPS improvements act as a performance multiplier in a hub and "spoke" architecture, which is why optimization of Klaytn's consensus mechanism to boost the TPS remains a commitment of the Klaytn team.

The latest update from Klaytn, on 23 December 2022, states that the network will evolve into an open blockchain ecosystem where anyone can act as a block validator if they meet certain qualifications while maintaining the existing Governance Council structure and roles. This shift aims to enhance business opportunities, profit-sharing structures, and network security while ensuring openness, transparency, and censorship resistance. Consensus algorithms will be improved to allow for the participation of as many validators as possible without compromising Klaytn's performance.

Any scaling endeavor will require extensive testing for obvious security reasons before it is implemented, which is why it is equally important to have the capability to keep up with the industry standard that is set by the Ethereum blockchain's tech stack.

Building on Top of The World's Blockchain

While the Bitcoin blockchain was meant to decentralize finance, Ethereum's aim is to decentralize the world; hence, its flexibility and limitless applications into real-world matters as discussed in previous chapters.

All that complicated tech that makes the Ethereum blockchain work is not something that is accessible to the common developer. As such, Klaytn's goal is to bridge that gap, targeting new builders who want to explore the metaverse as a platform for their projects.

With full compatibility with Ethereum-based software, a set of user-friendly tools enables new developers to build metaverse infrastructure, while

customized Layer 2 solutions, SDKs and smart
contracts, wallets, chain explorers, bridges, and oracle
support, regulate and connect projects to the
real world.

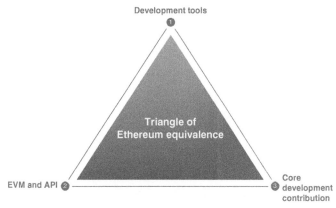

Source: Klaytn Light Paper: https://klaytn.foundation/wp-content/
uploads/Lightpaper.pdf

The Klaytn blockchain not only welcomes dApps,
but also any app that wants to leverage off blockchain
technology. It is not a must for dApps to offer
decentralized web services.

Whatever the project may be, from GameFi to
dApps, compatibility with Ethereum is always going to
remain a key factor for the foreseeable future. Tweaks to
Klaytn are often to complement Ethereum rather than
complicate an already busy blockchain. The aim is that

projects built on Klaytn can enjoy the same tech stack as Ethereum with a more user-friendly approach.

However, Klaytn's Ethereum equivalence goes beyond matching the blockchain giant's tech stack as Ethereum Improvement Proposals are a two-way conversation, meaning both Klaytn and Ethereum exchange ideas on how to improve the Ethereum blockchain, which once successful, will bring benefit to Klaytn as well.

Shared Governance of a Shared Ecosystem

After governing Klaytn under strict protocol for several years that saw stable growth, the blockchain is now incorporating a more decentralized structure to distribute power equally.

Decentralization is shared global vision and, thus, should be at the core of blockchains. Klaytn's amendments to its governing structure include having 30% of its Governance Council comprising DAOs – or a DAO of DAOs – to lead the blockchain's core development.

Planning to abolish the Gini Coefficient in Klaytn's voting algorithm to give DAOs in the Governance Council more influence as they grow and shifting Governance Council requirements to prioritize candidates who are committed opens new possibilities

in the direction that Klaytn could go in being an
all-inclusive blockchain.

Pushing toward greater decentralization, Klaytn
will be increasing its Governance Council to
50 members, with a focus on onboarding leading
DAOs, followed by network upgrades to double the
maximum number of Governance Council
members to 100.

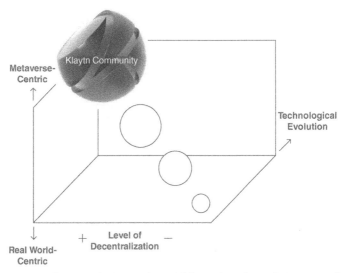

Source: Klaytn Light Paper: https://klaytn.foundation/wp-content/
uploads/Lightpaper.pdf

Shared governance by DAOs, builders, enterprises,
and institutions are the key to Klaytn's progress in as a
decentralized platform, as such Klaytn's governance

protocol does not allocate voting privileges to just anyone who holds KLAY, its native token.

Only those who are committed to actively developing and growing the Klaytn ecosystem are granted a seat on the Council. Validators must stake at least five million KLAY and Council members can have their stake slashed if they misbehave. To grow sustainably, new Council members are only confirmed after every 86 400 blocks are generated.

KLAY is used in various transactions both on and off Klaytn's blockchain, including with various projects connected to the Ethereum blockchain. To facilitate higher adoption, loyal users receive rewards in the form of KLAY tokens.

As of November 2022,[4] Klaytn mints 6.4 KLAY per new block and allocates a generous amount of its total emissions toward the development of its ecosystem – the breakdown: the Klaytn Governance Council Reward receives 50%, the Klaytn Growth Fund gets 40%, and the Klaytn Improvement Reserve 10%.

At time of writing (25 December 2022), Klaytn is ranked #64 by CoinMarketCap with a market cap of US$498 250 823 and a circulating supply of 3 069 022 085 KLAY coins.[5]

---

[4]https://medium.com/klaytn/klaytn-block-reward-adjustment-governance-proposal-vote-result-539be024f953
[5]https://coinmarketcap.com/currencies/klaytn/

In addition to Klaytn's continuous growth and quest for DeFi inclusivity, the chain's updated tokenomics reinvest 50% of newly minted KLAY.

Growing the ecosystem by incentivizing builders, funds are distributed via grants and rewards programs by the Klaytn Improvement Reserve to developers who create infrastructure, tools, and services that can improve the Klaytn network; by the Klaytn Growth Fund to reward promising early-stage projects based on Klaytn; and by the Proof of Contribution (PoC) program that recognizes builders of smart contracts that enable or simplify more on-chain activities to increase Klaytn's utility and KLAY's liquidity.

As a blockchain that was founded by the subsidiary of a software giant, Klaytn is as corporate-friendly as it is builder-friendly. Klaytn is looking to be the preferred blockchain for enterprises and enterprise-level use cases, and with industry titans such as Japan's GMO Internet Group, Indonesia's Salim Group, and mobile gaming leaders Netmarble and WeMade among its partners, Klaytn has the potential to achieve this.

There is a lot of hope for Klaytn, with its solid reserves and financial foresight and planning, the blockchain might just become a household name in years to come. But perhaps what is truly the cherry on top of this multi-layered cake is that Klaytn is also the official blockchain partner for Bank of Korea's Central Bank Digital Currency (CBDC) project, which will find its proverbial home on a private, modified version of Klaytn.

11 A Brave New World

It's true what they say: it gets lonely at the top. So, what does the future hold for the strongest nation in the world today?

With the United States dictating global trade through its sanctions and veto power, directly stirring the course of history for over half a century in its favor, the country does not have many friends.

The US's foreign policy has made a lot of enemies for the nation. Hostilities toward the United States will never end as long as it continues to bully other nations. However, the country is approaching a fork in the road.

Shoddy alliances from the Middle East to Europe are beginning to fall apart due to pressure from rising powers in Asia and parts of the Global South.

Meanwhile, the war in Ukraine that diminishes global food supply and disrupts Russian oil pipelines to

Europe has already caused a politically chaotic situation, including the election of three different prime ministers in the United Kingdom in this year alone (2022).

As the United States and its allies go up against a burgeoning East, more opportunities will arise to use blockchain as an equalizer in the face of unfair political pressure from both sides.

Alternative methods to settle payments will ultimately be used to bypass sanctions, which will become useless as economic warfare for central powers. Nations will no longer suffer from crippling economies brought upon by these instruments of monetary imperialism. International pressure will amount to the United States changing its policy to solely use sanctions on individuals such as dictators and top brass members of regimes, terrorists, and international criminals, instead of being used on an entire country's poverty-stricken population.

Particularly where Society for Worldwide Interbank Financial Telecommunication (SWIFT) is not prominent, governments and banks will use the blockchain to overcome distance issues, allowing about 1.4 billion people (according to the World Bank) to join the global Web 3.0 economy.

With last-mile connectivity issues in banking addressed, the un-banked will be able to participate in trade. Countries that once had to support these disparate communities will experience a boom in economic activity as a result.

An increase in global participation in trade will result in more demand for energy. The ongoing energy crisis has already tested the relationship of the United States with its closest ally in the Middle East: Saudi Arabia. The Organization of the Petroleum Exporting Countries (OPEC) will continue to put pressure on the United States as China and other rising industrial nations seek alternative currencies to purchase oil.

The Petrodollar will fall sooner or later, and the US dollar will lose prominence as the global currency of trade, but it will not be soon until or if complete dedollarization happens. The dollar is too entrenched in the global financial system at the moment for any significant change in trading currency.

However, the pressure on the Federal Reserve Bank to balance the US economy for the strength of the dollar to persist will prompt the nation to create its own Central Bank Digital Currencies (CBDCs). Even though the US government will do everything in its power to delay the degrading of the dollar's prominence and promise of stability, there will eventually be a digital dollar to facilitate America's entry into the developing digital market which could be worth as much as US$37 trillion by 2040, according to some

researchers, as reported by the World
Economic Forum.[1]

The United States is at yet another turning point in
history. It has the chance to redeem itself, to
acknowledge the role it played in the setting up and
destruction of various regimes, the politically motivated
sanctions it slapped on nations that place them at a
disadvantage, and the endless and pointless wars it has
fought based on "American interests."

The United States can join the world in fair trade
in the digital economy or it can do the opposite and
oppose the advancement of nations attempting to break
away from the dollar.

How the United States repositions itself will greatly
matter in the years to come. New alliances will be
forged, yesterday's bickering leaders will be tomorrow's
bromances, and vice versa. Politics will always be a
merry-go-round of blame and deceit, but at least we
should see more diplomatic decision-making when it
comes to larger nations negotiating terms relating to
world trade. With equitable distribution of power
among economic powerhouses, maybe one day, just
maybe, every nation in the United Nations would be
able to put aside past conflicts and be friendly with

---

[1]The dark side of digitalization – and how to fix it (World
Economic Forum): https://www.weforum.org/agenda/2020/09/
dark-side-digitalization/

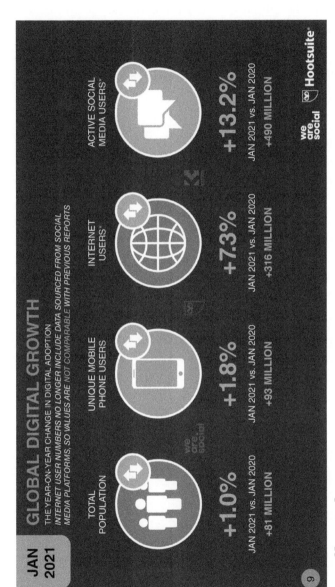

Source: Hootsuite Inc

each other, in terms of fair trade for the benefit of their economies and the people.

In the coming years, America could become the United States of Isolation once again, as it did when the nation sanctioned the whole world in the late 1800s, or it could drop the e-dollar into the basket of CBDCs that will become the next Bretton Woods and join the group of new currencies that would facilitate most of the world's trade.

I'm Still Walking, So I'm Sure I Can Dance

If what doesn't kill you only makes you stronger, then Africa is coming back with a vengeance.

Already singled out as the next booming economy, the continent is removing the remnants of colonialism such as the CFA, and introducing their own CBDCs for financial sovereignty.

5G broadband access will become cheaper with companies like Starlink entering the continent to capitalize on the market while it is still in its infancy. Wired to 5G connectivity, the digital gig or freelancer economy is expected to benefit the most, as with the service industry.

In the past, countries like China and Korea – manufacturing giants that have integrated themselves with the latest tech developments and innovations, with huge middle-class populations to test and support tech growth – had to go through an industrial phase to get where they are now.

Too much competition in industrial development would spell doom for the planet. Scientists and climate change researchers have predicted droughts that last for over 300 days annually in some parts of the world within the next 20 years. Conversely, rising water levels have been reported globally. Catastrophic events are on the cards if we do not take sustainability seriously.

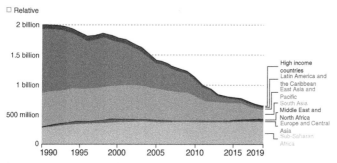

Source: World Bank/Bloomberg https://www.bloomberg.com/opinion/articles/2019-04-24/africa-s-only-way-out-of-poverty-is-to-industrialize

If Africa goes through a phase of industrialization with over-development of farming land and mining industries, the whole world will experience dire consequences. Brazil's Amazon rainforest that has been blazing for over a decade – most notably in 2019 when images of cauldron-black smoke turned midday into night in the city of São Paulo – is a prime example of what could happen should Africa industrialize in a traditional sense on a mass scale.

This does not need to necessarily happen if the Web 3.0 digital economy is adopted across Africa.

Access to credit will create a new middle class that will bypass this industrial phase. Access to the digital economy will give anyone with an internet connection the chance to be part of the new middle class.

Services that can be offered over the internet will blossom, and those who can integrate traditional skills with tech skills will be able to move forward. Education, communications, marketing and advertising, data analytics, programming, engineering, architecture, web design, bank services, and more, including established brands and multinational companies seeking employees, will soon be available on Web 3.0, making it the place to be to engage service providers around the globe.

New service platforms will arise, creating more higher paying jobs and a skilled labor force. This will lead to more use cases for all digital currencies in a Web 3.0 environment.

The fact that many nations are still standing today, despite centuries of foreign oppression, means that there's a chance that they will be dancing come tomorrow.

The First Days are the Hardest Days

It is still pretty much the Wild West for the decentralized finance (DeFi) movement today. There are over 20 000 blockchain projects that exist on the market, and there is not as much cooperation as there should be. In fact, most of these companies are in direct competition with each other for market share and dominance.

To tame the unpredictable frontier of blockchain fintech, tools for regulated growth must be put in place by governments and users of Web 3.0 platforms themselves.

It is crucial that the process of verification stays the way it was intended to be when Satoshi Nakamoto wrote the white paper that conceptualized Bitcoin and solved the Byzantium Generals Problem once and for all.

With CBDCs, we see governments attempting to co-opt the power of blockchain to capitalize on its capabilities and the metadata that follows.

Verification must always stay decentralized as central powers have the tendency to use our data against us. To deal with security effectively, our data needs to be decentralized as much as possible. As it is, there are already too many red flag cases that are allowed to proliferate freely online.

Catfishing, burner accounts, trolls, fake news, scams, and toxic behavior lurk at every corner of the internet of today and have led to disturbing trends such as recruitment for terrorist organizations and other extreme ideological groups.

Identity theft by hackers is rampant on social media as well. In the first quarter of 2022, Facebook took action on 1.6 billion fake accounts. While many believe that most fake accounts are bots created to execute malicious activity or at the very least, data hacking, a report this year by Tech News World claimed that a third of US-based social media users surveyed by USCasinos.com created fake accounts for various reasons.[2] It does not matter what information is displayed on a profile, anyone could be anyone.

Trust will always be at the center of everything. Without trust, we cannot move forward. Conversations on how to create decentralized trust for Web 3.0 economic activities will get more interesting as we strive to create a productive, efficient internet society.

Despite the lack of security at present, the internet has flourished as an alternative platform to conduct business and with the COVID-19 pandemic, work-from-home culture has accelerated. New web-based tools for various industries are being created every day

---

[2] A Third of US Social Media Users Creating Fake Accounts (Tech News World): https://www.technewsworld.com/story/a-third-of-us-social-media-users-creating-fake-accounts-176987.html

as the meaning of the New Normal evolves from being associated with lockdown-fueled paranoia to remote-work productivity.

Smart contracts on the blockchain that address the issue of trust will see added global GDP that will make China's double-digit GDP growth seem like a molehill.

Since initiating free-market reforms in 1979, China has been among the world's fastest-growing economies. When the country's GDP growth averaged 9.5% through 2018, the World Bank described it as "the fastest sustained expansion by a major economy in history" but it was nothing compared to China's 14.2% GDP leap in 2007.

China's GDP growth, on average, doubles every eight years and has so far helped to raise about 800 million people out of poverty. In addition to being a major commercial partner of the United States, China is also the largest foreign holder of US Treasury securities, helping Uncle Sam fund federal debt and keeping US interest rates low.

Now, imagine what would happen if all international trade barriers were removed, and every nation could trade freely without the interference of policies and regulations that stagnate GDP growths and isolate economies?

No economist can accurately predict or model the potential GDP of the world today, what more in the

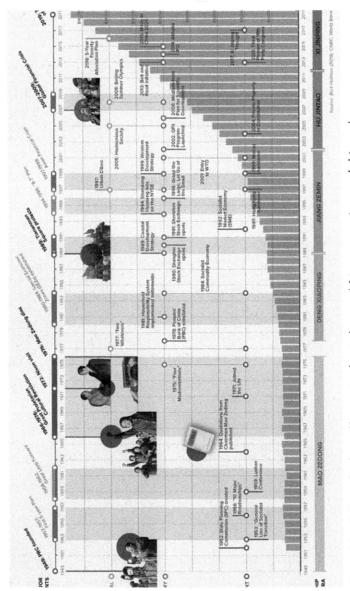

Source: Visual Capitalist https://www.visualcapitalist.com/china-economic-growth-history/

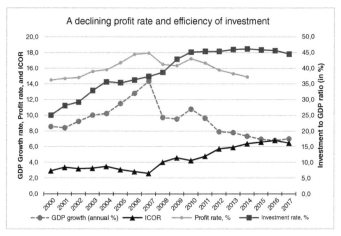

Source: CADTM https://www.cadtm.org/A-Little-History-of-Chinese-Economy

years to come? We are looking at a dynamic world where exchange of different forms of digital currency, whether CBDCs, cryptocurrencies, stablecoins or even NFTs, would be the norm in our daily routines.

You Speak My Language

The internet was officially born on 1 January 1983. Computer networks did not have a standard way to talk to each other before this. A new communications protocol, Transfer Control Protocol/Internetwork Protocol (TCP/IP), was created to enable interfacing among different kinds of computers on different networks.

This meant that all networks could now be connected by a universal language.

Much like how people today ignore the potential of blockchain to eliminate trust issues and prefer to focus on the daily highs and lows of cryptocurrency trading, the early internet was equally misunderstood.

At its infancy, the internet's potential led to hype and exaggeration which in term brought about the Dot-Com bubble burst of the early 2000s, just barely 20 years after the internet was conceived. Many people lost huge sums of money along the way and people today continue to get scammed, but there is no stopping the progress of web-based transactions. Life online will only continue to grow and so will the digital economy.

Various tech giants were, once upon a time, babies in a wild frontier. Today their share prices are among the most expensive on Wall Street and international exchanges, and their CEOs among the richest men in the world. But ask anyone who was using the internet when Facebook launched to the general public in 2006, and they would say that there were other similar social media platform competitors, and almost no one could tell the difference between them.

From the tens of thousands of blockchain companies that exist today, only a few will remain. Reputational evaluation will weed out the weak.

After years of assurance, the remaining blockchain companies with good track records will expand and even merge with each other. In the true spirit of decentralization, blockchain will continue to be a crowdsourced development.

Gas fees are currently required to support the current state of the blockchain ecosystem. As more developers get roped into the field, gas fees will go down and it might even be subsidized or free in the future.

Open blockchains will become a utility; something that people in cities and modern societies would need, like WiFi, to do business in the new world. Governments would want to support their local digital economies by reducing gas fees involved in certain transactions, like purchasing goods and services in support of local businesses and dealing with government-related transactions and taxes.

At some stage, the blockchain will be a standard part of the tech stack in any organization like the data cloud and servers we have today. The blockchain will be a crucial component in running any organization that involves seamless transactions.

In this future, the new generation of school-leavers will be confronted with complex decision-making chores, but they will be prepared. Just like how non-English speaking parents in the past knew that their children would have to learn English to be able to interact with the world, future generations will be pushed to take up coding.

Knowledge of the basis of coding would be something like the ability to converse in English in today's world. The higher one's level of proficiency, the easier it gets to move around and do business.

With the trend of humans having less physical interaction and more digital interaction, the new generation will be a generation that is able to interact with computers that have functions beyond what we can imagine today. At the moment, user experience (UX) might be structured in a way that is friendly to the computer-illiterate but the future of UX will see more complex interactions between man and machine.

Just like those who could not speak English were held back economically, the computer-illiterate will be unable to access the Web 3.0 economy of the future and hence, unable to move forward.

No one should be left behind in this future that we are working so hard to create. Fair trade must remain a basic human right, even though it is nowhere close to reality these days. It defeats the purpose of DeFi if the world has more disparity out of digitization. This is not the utopia we want.

It is important for us – you, me, anyone reading this book – to set the right tone in the decades and for the generations to come. Let the youth of tomorrow know that the world is still in their hands, that they still have the power to change it for the better just like how their parents, grandparents, and ancestors did.

Let us not fear the future because it is unknown but embrace it by getting familiar with it now.

As travelers in the journey of life we will come across many hurdles and roadblocks that will test our humanity. Remember to be kind.

There's a long way to go and a lot to do, but if we start now, the journey will be an interesting one.

Until then, just keep truckin' on. . .

INDEX

References to Figures will have the letter 'f' following the page number